Published in 2016 by
Laurence King Publishing Limited
361–373 City Road
London EC1V ILR
www.laurenceking.com

Text: Charlotte + Peter Fiell
Design: Sam Morley

A CIP catalogue record for this book is available from
the British Library.

ISBN: 978-1-78067-896-2

Printed in China

Samuel Chan

Design Purity + Craft Principles

Charlotte + Peter Fiell

Laurence King Publishing

Preface

Looking back, my becoming a furniture designer was a rare convergence of heart and mind. When I began the process there was not much else I wanted to do, nor that made sense for me to do. So I never doubted this was the life for me. I still wake up every day eager and excited to do my work, and for that I am profoundly thankful.

When Shirley and I were first married, our home was spartan for years until we could afford the pieces we really wanted. Good design, for me, is also a convergence of heart and mind: it makes sense to you when you first see it, and inspires affection in you the longer you have it. I hope my furniture designs might do the same. When a piece like that is passed on, it reflects not just the designer or maker, but also the user. Design then becomes an ongoing dialogue, and that's what I enjoy most: meeting all sorts of people and their giving me the opportunity to turn our dialogue into a piece of design that's particular to them.

In recent years a new interest in craft and its relationship to contemporary design has emerged. This was not always the case. In the early days of Channels, it was far from clear how our offering of original design with craft values would be received; people with the means to invest in furniture tended still to bank on traditional style. Against the flow, Charlotte and Peter Fiell championed contemporary furniture in all its guises and gave me one of my earliest breaks. Many years have passed and, in the day-to-day running of a business, one seldom reflects on the narrative of how one has got here. I am therefore very grateful to the Fiells for suggesting that they write this book. They have told the story in a way I never could. What emerges is that – along the way and often at critical points - I have been blessed with a loyal family, generous supporters and creative collaborators. To each and every one - thank you.

Samuel Chan

5

Contents

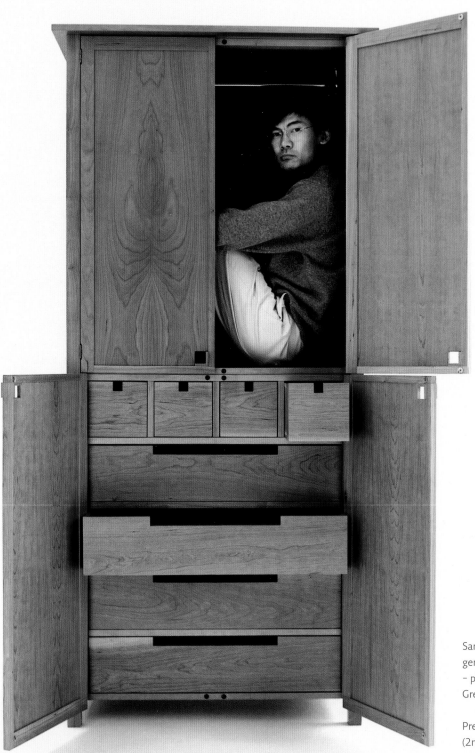

Samuel Chan inside his Alba
gentleman's wardrobe, 1998
– photographed by Adrian
Green

Previous spread: Alba chair
(2nd edition), 1995

Introduction

We first met Samuel Chan at a design exhibition held at the Royal Horticultural Halls in Pimlico, London, in 1988. Back then, stylish high-quality contemporary furniture was pretty thin on the ground, at least in Britain, with the prevailing taste being mainly for classicizing Postmodern statements *à la* David Linley, or reproduction antiques, with Biedermeier and the English country-house look being especially popular. Samuel's work was, in contrast, like a breath of fresh air, but over and above this what struck us most about his designs was their extraordinary level of craftsmanship. This was furniture that encapsulated the same craft ideals and innate simplicity found in Shaker furniture or Arts and Crafts Movement designs from the late nineteenth and early twentieth centuries. His stripped-down modern designs possessed an engaging purity that gave them a quiet and elegant sophistication – much like the work of Frank Lloyd Wright or Charles Rennie Mackintosh. Little did we realize then, that these pieces presaged the New Simplicity movement of the early 2000s. We could, however, see that this young designer–maker had a skill set way beyond his years and was one to watch. And that is exactly what we did and have done over the last two decades, and the more we have got to know Samuel's work the more impressed we have become.

After our first encounter, we met up with Samuel a number of times over the following few months and came to appreciate his highly considered approach to design. He struck us as a very thoughtful and honourable person, who was also a gifted designer. Rather like his designs, he conveyed a strong sense of focus and resolve, and listening to him talk about his work one was struck not only by his obvious love and feel for furniture-making, but also by his insightful understanding of how the furniture industry worked. It just so happened that we were in the process of opening a gallery on New King's Road, specializing in postwar and contemporary art and design, and so we invited Samuel to participate in one of our very first exhibitions entitled 'New Art and Design' held in October 1988. Included in this exhibition was his remarkable Curve chair that is, by anyone's standards a technical masterpiece of woodcraft. Over the next couple of years we also showed other designs by Samuel, most notably his Alba high-backed chairs (1989), with their distinctive pierced square-cut motif, often alongside work by the likes of Tom Dixon, Ron Arad, Ross Lovegrove and Danny Lane, who were then also young up-and-coming designers.

Samuel has since matured and developed into an exceptionally talented designer, as the numerous design awards he has received attest. One early design commentator described his designs as having 'an uncommon logic'[1] and certainly throughout his career his work has been guided by a strong belief in the ethics of craft principles and design purity, or, in other words, quality and simplicity. The way a designer chooses to approach problem-solving, for that is really what design is all about, is always very revealing for it offers a window into their soul. For the act of design is a powerful means of non-verbal communication that expresses the creator's hopes and desires, and is a reflection of their distinctive creative personality. To truly appreciate Samuel's work, it is helpful to understand how his character was formed by his early life experiences, for therein lies an explanation of his later motivations and goals as a designer. Put simply, to understand a designer is to understand his work, and this is especially the case with Samuel, for although his designs might appear to have an effortless simplicity, there is far more to them than immediately meets the eye. In fact, once you get to know Samuel, you realize everything he does is underscored by a deep moral philosophy, and that is ultimately what sets his work apart.

The Early Years:
Ancestry + Cultural Roots

Born in Hong Kong, Samuel's early childhood was far from privileged. Yet, despite its challenges, or maybe because of them, it equipped him with a strong work ethic, a sense of moral fortitude and a remarkable level of resourcefulness that has stood him in good stead during his adult life. His earliest memories are of living with his parents Mei Tak and Ruby Chan in his paternal grandparents' house in Rennie's Mill, or as it is now referred to, Tiu Keng Leng. During the mid-1960s and early 1970s, this ramshackle village on the east side of the Kowloon peninsula, which had evolved from a former refugee camp, was a world apart from the bright neon lights of high-rise Hong Kong Island and bustling Kowloon. It was essentially a Nationalist enclave, for the original tented camp had been set up by the British to specifically accommodate former Kuomintang (KMT) officials and followers who had fled to Hong Kong from mainland China, prior to the establishment of the People's Republic of China in 1949. In fact, both sets of Samuel's grandparents had been forced to escape mainland China when the Communists took power, his paternal grandfather because of his political associations, and his maternal grandfather because of his religious beliefs. His father's father, who came from Hubei province, had been a very high-ranking officer within the Nationalist Army but during the Chinese Civil War, while he was commanding one of the last KMT strongholds in China, he discovered much to his dismay that the Nationalist leader Chiang Kai-shek had already fled to Taiwan. Feeling utterly let down and realizing his untenable position as the Red Army advanced, he had no option but to also flee from China, with his wife and son in tow. As Samuel notes, 'Because they were located right in the centre of China, they were some of the very, very last people out.' Their journey overland was perilous for, had the Communists caught them, then in all likelihood they would have been executed. And they were by no means alone: in 1949 it is estimated that up to 100,000 Chinese refugees were flooding into Hong Kong each and every month[2].

Above: Samuel with his parents, Ruby and Mei Tak Chan, and his older sisters, Alice and Grace, 1971

Right: Samuel standing on a podium having come first in a race at St James' Primary School in Wan Chai, Hong Kong, 1976

Having lost everything, his grandparents, together with his father, finally arrived in Hong Kong in 1949 and were subsequently placed in the tented settlement of Rennie's Mill. Over the succeeding decades, Rennie's Mill became a very close-knit community, with the former refugees building their own homes there to form a permanent town. Ostensibly cut off from the rest of Hong Kong, with the only access being the sea or the narrow, steep and winding Po Lam Road, Rennie's Mill was such a hotbed of anti-Communism that it was often referred to as 'Little Taiwan'[3]. It was here that Samuel poignantly remembers when he was a small child, maybe four or five years old, standing in a long queue with his grandfather so he could collect his weekly welfare payment from a charitable organization[4] – it was an experience that inculcated from a very early age the desire for self-reliance. As he recalls of his grandfather, who had once been a high-ranking army official, 'He was a lost man who felt the whole world was against him.' This grandfather often received invitations to go to various dinners and events held by the Nationalist government in Taiwan, but always refused to go for he could never forget what he perceived as the perfidy of his former comrades. During his childhood, Samuel became very close to this grandfather, who would also frequently regale him with stories of how established the family had been in China before the Civil War and how, in contrast, very hard life had been as refugees who had landed in Hong Kong with literally nothing.

Likewise, Samuel's maternal grandfather also had a hugely formative influence on him. He was, unusually, a Chinese Presbyterian minister, presiding over a church in the port city of Qingdao in Shandong province, on China's eastern seaboard, during the late 1930s[5]. When China eventually fell to the Communists all religious practice was outlawed, and so Samuel's grandfather – a deeply committed Christian and church leader – was forced to flee to Hong Kong. Interestingly, Samuel's paternal grandfather also converted to the same strand of Christianity after settling in Hong Kong. And so, on both sides of his family – his mother's and his father's – there was a strong sense of Christian faith, which Samuel grew up with and even to this day still guides who he is and what he does. Indeed, it is not chance that some of Samuel's designs bear a striking resemblance to Shaker furniture, with its pared-down

formal language of design and beautifully crafted constructions, for both possess a strong spiritual purity.

While still an infant, Samuel and his two elder sisters (Grace and Alice) moved with his parents from his grandparent's home in Rennie's Mill to urban Kowloon. During this time, Samuel's father worked as a company administrator, while his mother worked as a local teacher. Eventually, when he was four years old, his mother was offered a much better post working as the head teacher of a kindergarten on Hong Kong Island and so the family moved into an apartment right in the heart of high-rise Hong Kong. The pace of life was now more frenetic. Yet it was also an invigorating experience, as Samuel recalls, 'My memory is of a dense, tightly packed place full of people of all different backgrounds – some from overseas, others from mainland China. And although it was a big mix of people who were constantly moving from one part of the city to another, they all shared a very strong work ethic. In fact, everyone was striving to find a way to establish their families.' The 1970s in Hong Kong was a period of unprecedented economic boom, which was full of opportunities that most people enthusiastically grabbed in order to better their lives. It was also a life of huge contrasts, from the glittering majesty of the Peninsula Hotel, with its famous fleet of Rolls-Royce limousines, to the makeshift, floating shantytown of desperately poor people living in perilously overcrowded houseboats in Hong Kong Harbour. Yet, in all sectors of Hong Kong society there was, as Samuel notes, a common culture of self-improvement and an optimistic belief that hard graft and clever thinking would lead to enhanced prosperity.

His paternal grandfather instilled in Samuel the belief that he must 'work hard, and do my very best' as it was the only way one would earn 'a position in life' – it was a lesson that Samuel, as a young boy, took completely to heart. Importantly, both sets of grandparents spoke Mandarin (now called Putonghua) to him rather than Cantonese (the southern dialect spoken in Hong Kong), and so Samuel learnt to write 'proper' Chinese more easily than other children growing up in Hong Kong. This educational advantage meant that Chinese became Samuel's favourite subject when he went on to junior school[6]. His younger sister, Marylois remarks that Samuel has always possessed a natural flair for

the Chinese language and is a consummate storyteller. As Samuel's wife and business partner, Shirley Wong helpfully explains, 'Cantonese is a rather colloquial dialect, constantly developing informal words or phrases that can't be formally written down, whereas Mandarin in its written form is regarded as "proper" Chinese.' Even after Samuel moved with his parents and sisters to Hong Kong Island, the strong emotional tie to his grandparents living in Rennie's Mill was maintained through regular family visits, which in turn kept up his knowledge of Mandarin.

Above: Samuel with Mr Harry Knock, the teacher who inspired him to pursue a career in furniture design and making, 2005

Moving to England: School Days + Early Creativity

In common with many Chinese families, the Chans possessed a strong belief in educational achievement, and this led Samuel's parents, who by this stage both had good, well-paid jobs, to make the momentous decision to move to Britain when he was at the point of transitioning from primary school to secondary school. They thought that by emigrating to the UK, it would mean Samuel would receive a better education than if they stayed in Hong Kong, where there was huge competition for good school places. At this stage Hong Kong was still a British colony, and his parents had visited Britain a couple of times in order to see various family members from his mother's side who had already settled there. It was these visits that spurred their decision to move to the so-called 'mother country' themselves. It meant resigning from their secure jobs, packing up all their worldly possessions, saying goodbye to their parents, relations and friends, and flying to a new country some 6,000 miles away. It was a remarkable leap of faith into the unknown. But before moving to London, Samuel's father made him solemnly promise to write a letter to his paternal grandfather in Chinese every fortnight without fail. And this is exactly what Samuel did when he got to England, with his grandfather sending his letters back to him with any corrections marked in red ink so he could keep up with learning how to write proper Chinese. It would prove to be an invaluable exercise as it meant that Samuel did not lose his knowledge of the language while growing up in Britain. It also allowed him to maintain his Chinese roots, despite becoming very much a Londoner over the coming years. As Samuel observes, 'As a kid, I never imagined China would open up, in fact nobody did at the time', but when this eventually happened in the 1980s, 'my knowledge of Mandarin proved very useful for doing business on the mainland'.

When the Chan family emigrated to Britain in 1979, Samuel was just 13 years old and had never been on a plane before. In fact he had never been outside Hong Kong before, and it was all a bit bewildering. On his arrival in London, his first impression was, 'Where are all the high-rise buildings?', and he recalls thinking that all the endless streets of terraced houses looked confusingly alike and that he would never make head or tail of the city's road system or find his way around. On their arrival, the Chan family settled in Wandsworth in South West London, and although his mother spoke some English already, his father struggled to master the language. It was not an easy time for the family, both financially and emotionally, but most especially for Samuel who had 'not one word of English' yet found himself dropped into a new and very different, and at times highly confusing, culture.

That autumn, Samuel was enrolled at Spencer Park School, a large comprehensive boys' school located in Trinity Road, Wandsworth. Despite the school providing extra English lessons, he found it, in his own words, 'very tough'. Barely able to understand basic spoken English, he was expected by his teachers to study the works of Shakespeare, as well as French, which was 'just one language too far'. He spent most of his time in such classes completely lost, which was disheartening for a student who had previously been at the top of his class in certain subjects. He did, however, find solace in his woodworking and design technology classes, which

he loved because he 'didn't have to speak English at all'. Fortuitously for Samuel, his woodworking teacher, Mr Harry Knock seemed to understand the difficulties he was experiencing and took pity on him. One day he cut out a rectangular piece of plywood and wrote on it, 'I can have this boy' and then signed it with a flourish and handed it to Samuel. From then on whenever Samuel had English literature or French lessons, he would show this 'get-out-of-class card' to his teachers, and they would let him bunk off to the carpentry workshop, where he would be taught how to make basic joints and use a lathe by the kindly Mr Knock.

In fact, Samuel spent much of his time at Spencer Park in woodworking classes, where 'everything was done by hand'. If you subscribe to Malcolm Gladwell's theory that it takes 10,000 hours to achieve mastery in a field, then certainly Samuel was well on his way to becoming a master woodworker while still a teenager. During this period, he made various small objects, as well as bookshelves and a rocking chair for his mother – his very first piece of proper furniture. Luckily for Samuel, given his interests, the O-level curriculum as it was then, allowed him to take various related vocational subjects, notably woodwork, metalwork, design technology, technical drawing and craft studies, alongside more academic subjects such as English, mathematics and physics. Like other boys at his school, Samuel also nurtured a dream of becoming a professional footballer – 'playing on the wing for Spurs' – and, while this never happened, it not only instilled in him a lifelong love of football, but also helped him assimilate into the British way of life.

Learning the Art of Furniture-making

With his strong educational bias toward designing and making, Samuel unsurprisingly decided to take design technology and woodwork for his A-level subjects. It was during his first year of sixth form, while eating lunch in the carpentry workshop with Mr Knock, as he so often did, that his mentor asked him, 'What do you want to do after leaving here?' Samuel without hesitation replied, 'I'd like to be a furniture designer.' Mr Knock then asked, 'Have you ever considered doing a furniture design course?' Samuel did not know that such a thing even existed. Two days later, Mr Knock gave Samuel a prospectus and an application form for the London College of Furniture (LCF). He subsequently applied to do a two-year diploma course there and was offered a place. Now part of the Cass School at London Metropolitan University, the London College of Furniture was then located in Commercial Road, right in the heart of the East End of London's furniture-making district. For Samuel, the college was a complete eye-opener for not only did it boast exceptional facilities, with every advanced wood-cutting and metal-processing machine you could possibly imagine, but it was also very well run by a team of highly skilled technicians. In fact, the teaching there was exemplary with a number of its alumni from around this time later going on to become well-known names within the design world, notably Terence Woodgate, Michael Marriott and Matthew Hilton, thanks in no small part to the excellent technical grounding in cabinetmaking that the college gave them. It was a vocational course and as part of their tuition the students visited a number of local furniture-manufacturing workshops. Crucially, these factory visits gave Samuel an early insight into the workings of the furniture industry. After completing his two-year course, he could have gone on to take a higher diploma at LCF, however, his tutor, David Copeland, took him aside one day for 'a talk'. As they chatted about Samuel's plans for the future, while walking up and down the college's stairs repeatedly, his tutor turned to him and said, 'Samuel, as your tutor I'd like you to continue here, but as a friend I really think you should do a BA elsewhere.'

Heeding his tutor's advice, Samuel went on to do an undergraduate degree in '3D Design in Furniture' at Middlesex University, in Enfield, North London. It was a three-year course with only 30 students accepted per year, with most of these having previously undertaken art foundation courses. Thanks to the hands-on training he had received at the London College of Furniture, Samuel had a much better grounding than most of his peers in cabinetmaking and the technical side of furniture-making. In contrast, most of them, having come from an arts background, were far more interested in the design of furniture than in its construction. Samuel found that being among this group of fellow students helped to considerably widen his scope creatively, as they placed much more emphasis on design development and concept proposals than he had previously encountered at LCF. The first year involved a set project, yet as Samuel notes, 'It was a very open pathway involving lots of sketches and models, and you were ultimately able to point yourself in the direction you wanted to go.'

While he was still a student at Middlesex, Samuel was actively involved in the youth group of the Chinese Church in London – then based in Chiltern Street in Marylebone[7] – and it was through this group that he met his future wife and business partner, Shirley Wong, in 1985. She was in her third year of an architecture degree at the Bartlett School of Architecture in London and they immediately hit it off, sharing many of the same interests and having the same pared-down aesthetic sensibility. In fact, Shirley was, if anything, even more of a purist than Samuel at this stage, and encouraged him to study the stark minimalism and elemental nature of Japanese design[8]. During his third year at Middlesex he designed and made his extraordinary Curve chair as part of his final project, which had a Zen-like simplicity. The design was cleverly based on the form of the Chinese character for 'girl' and consisted of only four elements, which all had exactly the same radius. Another of his final pieces was a sideboard that had a frame inspired by the form of traditional Chinese sedan chairs, with suspended side panels of cream canvas. Both these early pieces were based on precise mathematical proportions – a signature feature that would become increasingly emphatic in his later works.

During his final year at Middlesex, Samuel deliberated whether or not to continue with his education, for while he had managed to get by on a student grant for his BA, there was no such funding available for doing an MA. His parents were not in a position to help him financially, so the only way he could possibly continue his studies was if he won a scholarship. His mother, Ruby, encouraged him to apply for an MA, but told him to be realistic, saying, 'Leave it to God, He will provide for you. If you get a scholarship then continue with your studies, but if not then you'll just have to accept reality and get a job. Just trust in God's will.' At this stage there were only two MA furniture-design courses in the country, one at the Royal College of Art in London and the other at the Buckingham College of Higher Education in High Wycombe (now Buckinghamshire University). This latter course was far more vocational in aspect than the one offered by the RCA, and Samuel therefore applied to it feeling it would equip him better for a career within the furniture industry. Importantly, Samuel was awarded a full scholarship to study at 'High Wycombe', as the course is commonly referred to, which not only covered all of his course fees, but also crucially provided a small maintenance grant. The 14-month-long course provided him with the first-rate practical training that subsequently enabled him to become the skilled designer he is today. His tutor – Chris Cattle – was a furniture designer himself, and, as Samuel notes, 'The facilities were brilliant, while the college's technicians were very knowledgeable.' For centuries, High Wycombe had been the chair-making capital of England thanks to its abundant supply of beech from the surrounding Buckinghamshire woodlands. This meant that while he was studying there, Samuel was at the very epicentre of the British furniture-making industry and, consequently, became properly schooled in all its traditional expertise[9]. In fact, at that stage, many of the local furniture-makers were still heavily involved in the college and actively encouraged students to learn 'the trade', and ultimately that is exactly what Samuel did.

Balsa-wood models of furniture designed while at Buckingham University, High Wycombe, 1987–88

The Wem Workshop

In October 1987, some four weeks after starting his MA course, Samuel exhibited his undergraduate final pieces at the 'Direct Design Show' held at the Royal Horticultural Halls in London. It was here that we first encountered Samuel and his work, which led to us showing his work in our design gallery on New King's Road. It was also at this exhibition that he met Hans van Ek, a Dutch timber merchant, who was so impressed with the pieces on display that he asked Samuel to work for him. Worried that, by doing so, it might jeopardize his MA scholarship he sought advice from his course leader at High Wycombe, who was very excited that one of his students had the opportunity of actually working to a 'live brief' and advised him to 'go for it'. He suggested that if Van Ek sponsored all of Samuel's travel expenses and material costs, then it would not compromise his scholarship funding. And this is exactly what happened, much to Samuel's delight because it now meant that all his expenses were completely covered for the year, which was a huge relief. One of the reasons Van Ek was so interested in Samuel's work was that he had recently acquired the long-established timber business, Albert Isherwood & Company based in Wem, Shropshire[10], which had a large timber yard sited next to the town's station. He had the innovative idea of setting up a small furniture-making workshop attached to the yard, so potential customers could select the timbers they wanted and then have them transformed into bespoke furniture by a team of craftsmen. And Samuel's simple yet beautiful designs were exactly what he had in mind for this speculative enterprise. After agreeing to work together, the execution of Samuel's MA designs were effectively sponsored by Albert Isherwood & Sons, which set up a furniture-making workshop overseen by its most skilled maker, Mike France, for this purpose[11]. During the Easter holidays, Samuel spent two weeks in the Shropshire workshop working alongside Mike on a range of furniture pieces, including the first version of his high-backed Alba chair (1988), which had distinctive square motifs cut into its back. As Samuel would later explain, he not only really liked this motif

in the early days, but it also had a secondary function in that it made his design harder to copy as it was a technically difficult thing to cut precisely. Other designs from the Isherwood project would form the blueprints for his later Wem collection (1999).

The timing for this fledgling design-making venture, however, was not ideal, as the United Kingdom was tipping into a deep recession and, during the last term of Samuel's MA, with his final project being around 75 percent completed, his sponsorship from Isherwood ceased as the company went into receivership and, consequently, its workshop was closed. Despite this considerable set-back, Samuel managed to complete his project and, fortuitously, was able to keep the rights to his designs because Isherwood had not fulfilled its contractual obligations. Around this time, Mike remembers Samuel saying, 'Some time we'll work together again,' as though it was a given destiny. When these early degree pieces were shown for the first time no one could believe the quality of execution, with several people coming up to Samuel and saying, 'You must have the best furniture-maker in the country.' Over the coming years, Samuel maintained contact with Mike knowing he wanted to work with him again, if and when an opportunity arose.

After graduating from Buckinghamshire in 1988, Samuel immediately found a job working for Ezra Attia & Associates, an interior-design company that specialized in hotel projects. Based in Hampstead, London, it undertook very large commissions and, as part of the firm's design team, Samuel found himself working on a variety of prestigious projects – most notably the Lanesborough Hotel in London – all of which helped him to learn the ropes of the interior-design contract market. During the seven years he was at Ezra Attia, Samuel also found time to work with his fiancée Shirley Wong on a number of very small-scale bespoke commissions and exhibited his designs at a number of group shows including 'Sit '89' at the Business Design Centre, London, which we helped curate, and the 'British Craftsmanship in Wood' exhibition held at Cheltenham College in 1990.

Channels: Design–Make–Sell

In 1990, Samuel and Shirley were married in the village church of Hardington Mandeville in Somerset, where an aunt and uncle lived. As Samuel's sister Marylois recalls, the reception was a 'rather curious outdoor affair' being inspired by Shirley's love of nature. The young couple subsequently set up home in Putney and, although Samuel was working full-time for Ezra Attia, and Shirley was working for an architectural practice, they managed to find the time to continue undertaking small private commissions as well – often driving large distances between workshops and clients' homes during their 'free' weekends. They eventually decided that they needed to set up their own furniture company and have their own showroom, and so begun planning in earnest. In 1992, Shirley stopped working full-time to embark on an architecture PhD, and this consequently meant she had quite a bit more time to dedicate to the planning of their new furniture design–make–sell venture, which they had decided to call Channels, for obvious reasons.

One of the first things Samuel did after deciding to establish his own furniture business was to drive up to Shropshire to ask Mike France whether he would be prepared to set up a workshop and make furniture for Channels, according to Samuel's designs. Mike politely declined feeling it was too much risk to take on personally, and Samuel drove back to London full of despondency knowing that he really needed Mike's cabinetmaking skills to make a real success of the venture. During a three-hour drive back to London, he kept thinking, 'How am I going to make this work? I need a solution. If I don't have a workshop, how will I be able to control quality?' Finally it occurred to him that maybe Mike might come on board if he could somehow find a way of funding the opening of his own workshop. It was still before the widespread use of mobile phones, so Samuel had to wait agonizingly to get back to London before calling Mike. The moment he arrived home, he picked up the phone and asked: 'Would you come and work for me as a manager if I set up a workshop myself?' Much to Samuel's delight,

Mike agreed, saying, 'Yes, that's fine, that'd work!' The only problem was Samuel now had to find a way of financing a workshop.

By pure chance, and completely out of the blue, one of the Chans' friends, Henry 'Hank' Tsang telephoned Samuel a few days later to say he was in London and would love to meet up. A successful American-Chinese investment banker, Hank had originally met Samuel in London but, by then, was based in Hong Kong. Over lunch they talked about Samuel's vision of establishing a furniture company with its own workshop and showroom. After listening to Samuel's design-make-sell plan, Hank turned to him and said, 'Why don't you count me in?' A few weeks later, having mulled over Hank's proposition, Samuel went over to Hong Kong and after chatting together decided to take up his offer. Acting initially as a sleeping partner, Hank was hugely supportive during Channels' first 'very tough' year or so, fondly describing it, as 'his hobby'. Every couple of weeks, he phoned up to ask, 'How's business?' and then Samuel would give him the low-down. Sometimes, a few days later, Samuel would find, much to his relief, that Hank had wired some surprise funds into the company's bank account. Crucially, because of his background in finance, Hank knew just how essential cash flow is to any business in start-up mode, and would say to Samuel, 'If you need it, use it, and if you don't, then just keep it in your account.' Hank was also able to offer invaluable and practical business advice that helped the Chans immensely during this early gestation stage of the business. As Samuel reflects, 'I couldn't have had, or still have, a better friend, or a better partner.'

In early 1995, after looking for several months, Samuel and Shirley finally spotted a suitable building at 3, New King's Road, which had formerly been an upholstery workshop. It seemed to them to be a good location to launch Channels, for it was close enough to the bottom of King's Road with its cluster of interior design and antiques shops, yet also within their affordability range. They subsequently bought the dilapidated Victorian building, situated on the ever-busy corner where King's Road turns into New King's Road. It had both dry and wet rot, and probably a hundredweight of metal tacks embedded in its floor, yet they slowly managed to transform it into a beautiful yet simple modern gallery

space. It proved to be a very complicated renovation, especially as they also extended the premises, but somehow they managed to work through all the various planning restrictions and party-wall issues, and in November 1995 the showroom was finally opened. It subsequently became Samuel's all-important 'window on to the world'. In parallel to the setting up of the showroom, and as agreed with Mike France, Samuel also opened that same year a small furniture-making workshop in Wem, Shropshire, with Mike as its manager. Both recall the excitement of taking delivery of all the different woodworking machines, which they had managed to purchase secondhand from here and there, and finally getting the workshop up and running to produce the first Channels pieces. This meant that by the time Channels opened for business in late 1995, its manufacturing capability was already well in place and ready to go, meaning Samuel could now focus his energies on designing new furniture for the showroom and winning all-important private commissions.

Having already resigned from Ezra Attia, Samuel now dedicated all his time to the new enterprise and, despite having very limited retail experience, from day one there was a steady stream of commissions. The reason was that Channels was offering something completely new and different: a bespoke design service whereby clients could sit down with Samuel and explain exactly what they needed and he could design it specially for them. As Samuel's sister Marylois, who joined Channels in 1995, explains, 'No one else was doing that then – not in contemporary furniture design – so Samuel managed to capture a large sector of this market.' One of his earliest clients was the musician Eric Clapton who purchased numerous pieces for his

various residences. Like the bespoke design service being provided by Channels, the type of furniture Samuel was offering had a refreshing difference too. With their East-meets-West look, these designs fused a very English craft sensibility with an Asian formal aesthetic, which was perfectly in tune with the new desire for less cluttered living spaces as well as the more international zeitgeist of the mid-to-late 1990s. Given his background in hotel design, Samuel often conceived his designs as mix-and-match room sets, which proved to be a winning formula as not only did corporate specifiers like being able to buy in a complete look, so did domestic customers too. His debut Alba collection launched at '100% Design' in 1996, included a slightly altered version of his earlier high-backed chair and a matching chest with seven drawers. Traditionally, a chest-of-seven-drawers is known as a 'semainier' as it has a drawer for every day of the week, or *semaine* in French. Yet despite this historic inspiration, Samuel's chest was far from traditional and revealed his almost obsessive interest in precise mathematical proportions. Likewise in its construction, while built on the craft traditions of English furniture making with its beautifully executed mortice-and-tenon and dovetail joints, it was at the same time a thoroughly stripped down essentialist design. His follow-up Memory collection (1997), in contrast, looked back to the historical furniture-making traditions of the East for inspiration, as its name suggested. Rather than exploring the furniture-making culture of Japan as other Western-based designers had done before, however, Samuel instead went back to his Chinese roots, and looked at pieces from the Ming dynasty – arguably the period that marked the highpoint of Chinese art and culture.

Significantly, like his earlier Alba collection, the Memory pieces, which comprised two chairs, two cabinets and various tables, were similarly distinguished by a strong sense of symmetry and proved to be extremely popular among Samuel's clients because they mixed so well with both modern pieces and Oriental antiques. Importantly, by the late 1990s prevailing taste was now catching up with Samuel and Shirley's East-meets-West minimalist-craft look, and although, as Marylois notes, the 'Zen label had never been an intent', it somehow stuck. With the inherent elemental simplicity of Samuel's furniture and his uncluttered sparse interiors featuring beautiful solid wood pieces set against pure white walls, there was an almost ethereal aspect to his work. Even as a young designer starting out, Samuel had been inspired by the work of Le Corbusier and Eileen Gray, whom he admired for challenging the design status quo with their revolutionary yet chic proto-minimalist designs during the 1920s and 1930s. It is interesting to note that neither of these designers had ever subscribed to the hard-core utilitarianism of their peers at the Bauhaus. Similarly, unlike most minimalists working in the late 1990s, Samuel's work was not defined by a hard-edged sterile coldness. In contrast, it was actually characterized by a sense of emotional warmth that cleverly humanized the all-too-often stark purity of minimalism.

Expanding Horizons + Prestigious Commissions

Realizing that most Londoners are pretty tribal when it comes to going outside their specific chosen locale, with West Londoners almost never venturing north of Hyde Park, and vice versa, Samuel and Shirley decided to open a second showroom in Hampstead Village in North London in 1998. Samuel already knew the area well, thanks to having worked there while with Ezra Attia, and was cognizant that its inhabitants had a similar socio-economic and cultural profile as his existing clients in West London. He was proved right, because although the Hampstead showroom was relatively modest, business was extremely good right from the start. This second 'window on to the world' enabled Samuel to capture a sector of London's interior design market that would never have thought of venturing to World's End in Chelsea, and certainly not to New King's Road, which would have seemed to them like the furthest reaches of the Wild West. Running two showrooms on different sides of the capital, however, proved very physically demanding and, as Shirley recalls, during this period, 'there was no such thing as weekends'. Added to this, the Chans were still living in Putney, which meant the inevitable hour-plus drive to and from Hampstead each day was taking its toll on family life, especially now that they had a young son,

Jasper, who was born in 1999. That same year, Samuel had also designed his extensive Wem collection, which would go on to define the Channels signature look: clean-lined simplicity with an underlying craft refinement.

After two years of running the two shops, the building next to the original showroom in New King's Road came up for sale. Both Samuel and Shirley felt it was the perfect opportunity to consolidate and have what they had always wanted for Channels: a double-shop gallery. Closing the Hampstead showroom, the Chans then 'took a big gamble' and purchased the adjoining building on New King's Road in 2000. Over the coming months, Shirley carefully project-managed the necessary renovations so that there was as little disruption as possible within the still-operating shop. Meanwhile, Samuel launched his uber-minimalist Zac collection (2000), which reflected a new kind of narrative within his work as it was conceived, first and foremost, as a dream-like room set for a fictional man called Zac who did most of his thinking in bed. The influential fashion retailer, Joseph Ettedgui, who had already shown Samuel's work in his eponymous store in Brompton Cross in Kensington, was so taken with this visually light collection made from English sycamore that he commissioned one of the four-poster beds especially for his daughter, Gigi. Around this period, Joseph's wife Isabel, who was then the creative director for the high-end leather goods company Connolly, showed a number of Samuel's pieces in the company's wonderful shop, then located on Conduit Street in Mayfair. Importantly, the Zac collection received heaps of press interest because it was just so ethereal-looking and photographed so beautifully, which boded extremely well for the planned showroom expansion.

Eventually, in the summer of 2001 the existing showroom was closed for the whole of August, so that the contractors could finally break through the walls between the two buildings and create a single, large open-plan space. This new showroom marked a new chapter in the story of Channels for it meant that Samuel now had plenty of room to show new work alongside his existing portfolio of designs. Since 1996, Samuel has created, virtually every year, a new collection to launch in London every September.

Left: Channels studio/
showroom in New King's
Road, London

Normally, Samuel spends a couple of months during the early part of each year coming up with ideas for the new furniture collection. He then tries to finalize these design concepts by April, thereby allowing sufficient time for his workshop in Wem to make up the pieces and then get them professionally photographed before their official launch in late summer. Given that each year meant the launch of a new collection, by 2001 Channels had already quite a significant number of designs in its portfolio, and the newly expanded three-floor double-fronted showroom in New King's Road enabled Samuel to show more examples from each range, while also having the space to display more experimental pieces too. That same year also saw Channels exhibit its designs at ICFF (International Contemporary Furniture Fair) for the very first time. Held in New York City, this major annual trade show enabled the company to reach a new American audience, leading to increasing commissions from across the Atlantic.

The Fusion Look +
Low-key High Style

During the late 1990s, Samuel had found himself increasingly taking on the role of a manufacturer for other companies too – supplying furniture to a number of leading design firms, including Conran, Heal's and Liberty. As business picked up, so did the need for greater manufacturing capacity, as there was only so much furniture the workshop in Wem could reasonably produce. Around this period, Samuel also kept getting approached by interior designers to design furniture for hotels and, time and again, he would go to the trouble and considerable expense to make up 'sample rooms' for them. But each and every time, he did not get the commission for, as the interior designers' would explain, 'we love the quality, but not the price'. He eventually realized that the interior designers were using him to establish a quality benchmark for other cheaper manufacturers to follow, most of whom were producing their furniture in Eastern Europe.

One night, Samuel explained the frustrating situation over supper to his father, who turned to him and said, 'If you want to do hotel furniture then you'll need to look into having production in China. You've got to realize you are not just a furniture designer anymore, you are also a manufacturer and you have to now think like a manufacturer.' Samuel's immediate reaction was that it would not be possible, because he could not think of how such an operation could come about. His father, who had already semi-retired, however, relished the idea of the challenge and soon afterwards set out on a fact-finding journey to China. This resulted in the founding of new production facilities in southeastern China in August 2000. Samuel's father masterminded the operation and then 'basically shouldered everything' for the next ten years. Over this time, he became a father figure to a 100-strong workforce[12]. He was always highly concerned that his workforce were looked after properly, telling Samuel, 'You've got to make sure they eat well, stay well and always get paid absolutely bang on time, for if you care about them, then they will care about you'[13]. This principled stance involving not only the provision of good working conditions but good living conditions too, has meant that the vast majority of workers have stayed the course from day one and, over time, their furniture-making skills have become considerably honed through proper training. Importantly, by providing meaningful work for its skilled craftsmen, the beautiful results of their labours undoubtedly give them the immense satisfaction of a job well done. And when workers take pride in their work, it always shows.

By taking over responsibility for the production of Samuel's simpler mass-produced pieces and the designs created for 'high-volume' hotel projects, when maybe 300 bedrooms need to be furnished with multiple different pieces of furniture, the production facilities in China hugely increased Samuel's capacity. This meant that the Wem workshop could now focus entirely on doing what it did best: executing high-end contemporary pieces – either for the Channels collections or as bespoke one-off commissions – that were highly reliant on the employment of traditional cabinetmaking skills. Around the turn of the millennium, special custom-made pieces became a rapidly growing sector of Channels' business, as

those who could afford it now tended to want to buy bespoke design solutions tailored to their specific individual needs. In fact, throughout the early 2000s Samuel just got busier and busier: not only was he designing pieces for the Channels showroom, and working on private commissions, but increasingly he was also engaged on large-scale interior-design projects too. One of his earliest hotel-furniture commissions was The Trafalgar in London, which boasted 129 bedrooms. This was followed, in 2003, by two more design-and-make commissions, one for a lawyers' chamber in Middle Temple and the other for a mission centre and bible college for COCM (Chinese Overseas Christian Mission) in Milton Keynes[14]. Soon, other prestigious commissions from abroad followed, including the Public Restaurant in New York City and the Kong Fok Church in Hong Kong, with both these projects reflecting Samuel's signature fusion look – an Oriental–Minimalism–Craft style. But it was his design and manufacture of furniture for the upper echelons of the hotel industry that really made Samuel's reputation. Whether it was the refurbishment of 'an established icon with a legendary reputation', or 'a confident newcomer intent on providing a different experience', the Channels studio under Samuel's direction managed to create an environment – whether classical or contemporary – that expressed the unique personality of each hotel. Unlike so many designers of hotel furniture, Samuel was able to give each and every project a special sense of place, while working hand-in-hand with the client's own interior designer. One early client, the Malmaison & Hotel du Vin Group, was so delighted with the work Samuel undertook for its Malmaison London hotel in 2003, that it went on to commission work for a further 21 different boutique hotels across the UK.

As Marylois notes, 'Samuel has always thought a lot about his clients, and during the era around the millennium he identified a new pattern of buyers. Many were highly successful bankers who were enjoying the rewards of the financial boom in the city and liked the idea of specially commissioning pieces. They realized they could express their individuality by having workspaces and living spaces that looked different from everyone else's.' In many ways it was, as Marylois puts it, 'a means of being distinctive'. Most of these

individuals did not come from the upper classes or aristocracy and therefore did not have a predilection for the stuffy old-school country-house look, yet nor did they want to appear *nouveau riche*, with anything too flashy. Samuel's designs were in many ways perfect for this new breed of patrons for they worked as 'luxury indulgences' – they had an inherent understated look, yet at the same time they were constructed from beautiful matched woods using precise proportions and superlative craftsmanship. In essence, these pieces were low-key yet high-style designs for the culturally savvy who wanted to use their wealth to acquire pieces with which they could emotionally connect.

Faith + Family

Crucial to its success in this area, Channels' design-make-sell remit meant Samuel could ensure that each and every piece that left his workshops met his high quality-control standards. Because no part of a design's manufacture was being subcontracted out, it ultimately meant everything was under his personal control, and Samuel is a real stickler for detailing. As anyone who knows Samuel well will tell you, he can actually be a bit of a disciplinarian when its comes to the execution of his designs because he wants them to be absolutely perfect. He refuses to compromise on the quality of the materials used or the construction methods employed because he is not just making furniture for the here and now, but for decades or even centuries to come. 'People are always asking me about the green credentials of our furniture,' Samuel says. 'And, undoubtedly, that heightened awareness of environmental impact has led to interesting innovations in design. Of course we need to take care how we source our materials, but for me the best, and least contrived, way of approaching the issue is to help consumers make sound, confident design decisions, and invest in furniture they won't want to throw away after a few seasons.' Put simply, Samuel's goal is to create timeless designs, which will function as the heirlooms of tomorrow, being handed

Bespoke hotel furniture
designed for Malmaison
London, 2003

A New Formal Language

down from one generation to the next. And in order to achieve this, by necessity, design thoughtfulness and manufacturing excellence are of paramount concern to him. As his wife Shirley notes, 'His faith does influence his work. And his entire style has evolved, I think, from his wanting to impose a sense of permanence to his designs – something that stems from his belief in the eternal.' For instance, the case pieces of his Tot collection (2003) for children were designed specifically to grow with the child, and then be used as 'adult pieces' once they had grown up.

Family life is also hugely important to Samuel, and Channels has always been first and foremost a family-run enterprise. With Samuel working closely with his wife Shirley and youngest sister Marylois on all aspects of the business, as the latter notes, 'We all muck in, and no roles are defined. We just get on with it like in any traditional family business.' Certainly Shirley has always acted as Samuel's 'sounding board and most astute critic', while overseeing the company's creative output, and Marylois – who previously worked as a journalist in Hong Kong – mainly concentrates on the marketing and PR side of things, as well as running the Channels showroom. Yet everyone's role is very fluid. More recently the Chans' eldest son, Jasper, has also been helping out his parents on their stands at trade fairs, while their youngest son, Tobias, is showing signs of following in his father's footsteps, having inherited his love of woodwork – much to his father's pride. As previously mentioned, Samuel's father was also heavily involved in the manufacturing side of the business, overseeing production in China right up until his death in 2010. This increased production capacity was very important for the subsequent evolution of Channels because it offered the opportunity to speculatively explore new manufacturing techniques – such as moulded plywood for his Flyt chairs – that enabled Samuel to ultimately up the volume of production on certain lines.

Around 2007, with the workshop in Wem and the larger facilities in China both established and investments made in new woodworking machines, Samuel was able to experiment with a new formal vocabulary based on curved shapes. Prior to this, Mike France and the Wem workshop had been creating pieces that had a very strict and straight geometry, but now Channels 'was able to do curves'. The Motley collection, of 2007, consequently marked a new departure both aesthetically and conceptually. The new machines prompted Samuel's design of 'drums', functional versatile tables/stools made of laminated sheets of bent plywood, while increasing contacts with different suppliers enabled him to explore new materials and processes. Also, the collection was markedly different in that it was not themed around a conceptual room set, as most of his previous collections had been, but was rather a coming-together of diverse design concepts that Samuel had been developing. It was, quite simply, a 'motley collection' of deceptively simple designs that were exquisitely detailed and shared a strong sculptural confidence. This sculptural quality became even more emphatic with the launch of the Motley II collection the following year, which included a dining table and coffee table that combined a very modern man-made material (Corian®) with a very traditional material (solid oak). Awarded a British Design Guild Mark, these pieces revealed in their beautiful constructions, which included exposed tenon joints joining the two materials together, that high-quality craftsmanship could be used effectively to create very simple designs that possessed an innate timeless quality. The Motley II collection also included a bookcase, wardrobe and sideboard. These pieces, with their rounded corners, had a more soft-edge minimalist look than his previous designs. It was, however, in the Motley III collection of 2009 that Samuel really hit his sculptural stride with three very different but equally aesthetically strong designs: his Motley floor lights with their Chinese lantern shades made from strips of hand-cut oak veneers that rest on their solid wood trunk-like stands; his award-winning Motley pallet drawer system,

which is an ingenious stack of drawer units that can be configured according to the user's needs; and his Egg chair, made from a block of laminated ash using a lathe and chisel, that acts as a functional artwork.

Around this time, as a way of expanding its reach, Channels made its Milan debut in April 2011, showing in Zona Tortona as part of 'designjunction', a collective of British designers, during the week of the famous Salone del Mobile. As Samuel recalls, 'That first year, ten British companies went and there was a real team spirit among the designers taking part.' Since these relatively small beginnings, 'designjunction' has grown to now include some 200 companies at each show, with Channels being regularly among them. Importantly, the collaborative experience of going to Milan with other likeminded designers prompted Samuel to think about finding alternative ways of working together in the future.

Joined + Jointed

Despite the increasing recognition and awards Samuel had been getting for his designs, the recession, which started in 2008, forced him to think deeply about the future direction of the company. Having worked so hard over the preceding ten years to establish the workshop and grow production capacity, he was determined to find new ways to make best use of these rare assets and keep his craftsmen working creatively. At the time, the instability of the global economy meant many hotel projects were put on hold. While these large-scale contracts had contributed significantly to the company's growth, Samuel had long been aware that he could not rely on them indefinitely: 'I was always grateful for these projects, and collaborated so well with some of our clients that they became friends, but

Top: Gillespie side tables, 2011

Bottom: Trident sofa designed by Simon Pengelly, 2013

25

the industry was changing, understandably.' Furnishing budgets within the hotel sector were diminishing, which meant margins were becoming too low for viability. While he was confident that the economy – and the projects – would bounce back, there was a more fundamental reason driving his rethink: 'I wanted to find a way forward in which we could drive some reasonable volume through our production, but by making furniture we're excited about, and in a way that allows us to control the design and the making totally, and marketed in a way that reflects the current situation.'

Despite the economic downturn, Samuel felt there was an opportunity in the shift of furniture retail towards direct selling on the Internet. The rise of online retail was a moment that needed to be seized: 'I realized that we were ideally placed to operate online: since day one we've been the designer and the manufacturer. While other companies struggle to "cut out the middleman", we've never had to deal with a middleman. We just needed to find a way to do design–make–sell – what we've always done – but on a larger scale.' Quality and pricing were the key factors: his ambition was to sell good-quality, well-made furniture at affordable prices under his own label to an entirely different and younger demographic than had previously made up his Channels clientele. Over the years, while exhibiting at various design shows, Samuel kept noticing that there was huge interest in 'really good design, but all too often it was too expensive for most people to afford' – whether it was his own Channels pieces or those of other high-end, design-led companies. He also knew a number of designers, often with a similar craft background to his own, whose work he admired yet who had had mixed success within the mainstream market because their commitment to craftsmanship was not compatible with affordability.

Utterly committed to Channels and the reputation for design purity and craft principles it had established, Samuel realized that any online enterprise needed to be a totally different and separate entity – yet at the same time have the same underlying ethos. If he could marry good-quality craftsmanship with simple, unadorned design then, in theory, he should be able to offer the online consumer something totally different and better value for money than other companies selling furniture over the Internet, many of which rely on selling licensed re-editions or, worse, pastiches of design classics. He also liked the idea of a collaborative venture, whereby all the designers he had become friends with over the years and who shared the same craft ideals, would contribute their designs alongside his own work. With this in mind, Samuel contacted the various designers he wanted to work with. Most of them were established British designers – Alex Hellum, Simon Pengelly, Rod and Alison Wales, and Freshwest – then there was the American-born, Milan-trained designer Sean Yoo and the respected Danish industrial designer Henrik Sørig. All of them were enthusiastic about his online retailing plans. Eventually, in 2013, Joined + Jointed (J+J) was officially launched at 'designjunction', during the week of the London Design Festival, as 'a new and unique collective of established and emerging designers brought together by a love of new ideas and meticulous craft'. Essentially, Samuel acts as the curator of J+J and oversees the production development of all the designs from initial concept to final finished product, bringing his artisan production knowledge to bear on each and every piece, regardless of whether it is his own design or by one of the other designers in the J+J collective. And, while it is still early days, Samuel is encouraged by the steady growth in sales that J+J has already experienced, which will undoubtedly increase once word gets out more widely about this new online retailer of really well-designed and beautifully crafted furniture.

In 2013, Samuel essentially took a year out to establish Joined + Jointed, and for the first time did not launch a new collection for Channels during London's September design season. The following year, however, with J+J up and running, Samuel went back to his roots, creating a new and highly bespoke range of furniture for Channels: the Kerning collection. This new range featured an exquisite level of detailing and emphasized more than ever Samuel's preoccupation with working out perfect proportions. Its name – Kerning – alludes to the carefully considered spacing between lettering used in typography.

The Goal of Complete Design Integrity

More recently, to mark the twentieth anniversary of Channels in 2015, Samuel decided to 'do something very sculptural and visually impactful'. The result was two of his most iconic designs to date: the monumental Column bookcases and his remarkable Magnus chair, both of which are masterpieces of woodcraft. The former design has a towering scale and a visual weightiness, which sets it apart from Samuel's earlier and more ethereal-looking pieces. It is as though as a designer Samuel has learnt all the rules and is now enjoying mixing them up. And despite the Column's almost totemic presence, it has an inherent playfulness too. It quirkily appears to defy the laws of gravity, with its stack of open-ended boxes placed precariously on top of each other to create a curious shelf structure that looks like it could topple at any moment, while in actual fact it is a surprisingly solid and functional piece of furniture. In the same way, the Magnus chair also pays 'homage to what Channels is all about' and playfully pushes the boundaries of cabinetmaking, with its tall back being made from a complex lattice of interconnecting pieces somewhat reminiscent of a Chinese puzzle. It is a time-consuming piece to make that revels in and also challenges the skill of the craftsman who has to build its back and seat sections from a plethora of different sized pieces, each shaped slightly different from the rest. With its complicated construction it is, of necessity, a high-value seating design, and with its strong and distinctive East-meets-West aesthetic it functions as usable 'design-art', which is exactly what Samuel intended it to do. With its highly distinctive silhouette, it has already become a modern-day iconic design, which signals an exciting new direction for Channels.

After two decades of perfecting the art of furniture-making, Samuel now enjoys the freedom to explore new creative avenues with his two very different ventures, Channels and Joined + Jointed, the former involved in crafting bespoke high-end and experimental pieces and the latter producing simple yet beautifully made everyday pieces. And, while these two entities are producing furniture that is at either end of the furniture-making industry scale, the designs all share the same strong design-DNA. In a period of cultural relativism, it is refreshing to find a designer with strongly held convictions about what is 'right' with regards to design and manufacturing practices. Or, if you like, he has a moral code to guide him. Above all, Samuel's work is a powerful testament to his unwavering faith in design purity and craft principles, or in other words, the pursuit of integrity. And as for the future, Samuel observes, 'Of course we want to grow, but we've always been conscious of not running ahead of ourselves. I want our growth to be steady but sure, and based on integrity, which for me is an undivided or unbroken completeness or totality.' This is the goal of a remarkably honest designer who has an exceptional sense of higher purpose, both in his life and in his work. And as a result, the quality of his work speaks for itself.

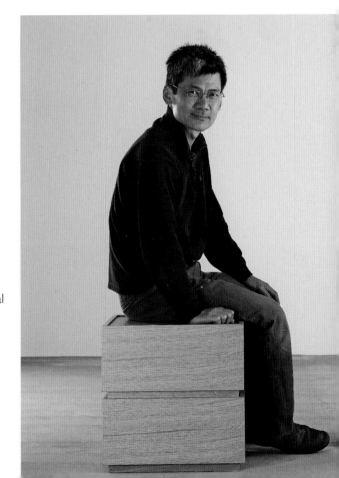

Biography

1964	Born 9 October in Hong Kong to parents Mei Tak and Ruby Chan
1979	Chan family emigrated to London from Hong Kong
1979-1982	Samuel Chan went to Spencer Park School, Trinity Road, Wandsworth, London
1984	B. Tech. Diploma in Furniture Studies (LCF Award with Credit), London College of Furniture
1985	Met Shirley Wong, who was then still studying architecture at The Bartlett School of Architecture, University College London
1987	BA (Hons) in 3-D Design, Middlesex University
1987	Awarded MA scholarship to study at Buckinghamshire University
1988	Designed his first version of the Alba high-backed chair
1988	MA in Furniture Design, Buckinghamshire University
1988-1993	Worked as a designer for Ezra Attia & Associates, London, undertaking numerous hotel interior-design projects
1990	Samuel Chan and Shirley Wong married at St Mary's Church, Hardington Mandeville, Somerset, UK
1995	Founded Channels and opened showroom at 3 New King's Road, London, UK; Samuel Chan's younger sister, Marylois, joins Channels
1995	Set up cabinetmaking workshop in Wem, Shropshire, UK, with Mike France as the workshop's manager
1998-2001	Founded and operated second Channels gallery at 84 Heath Street, Hampstead Village, London, UK
1999	Eldest son, Jasper, born
2001	Expanded Channels showroom in Chelsea so that it now included 1–3 New King's Road
2003	Second son, Tobias, born
2007	First Motley collection launched, signalling an exploration of new forms and production processes
2012	Three Wise Men pendant lights launched
2013	Founded 'Joined+Jointed' to manufacture and retail online furniture designed by himself and other designers
2015	New sculptural direction marked with the launch of Magnus chair and Column bookcases
2015	Samuel Chan named Furniture Designer of the Year at *Homes & Gardens* Design Awards Made a Freeman of The Worshipful Company of Furniture Makers

From top to bottom:
Samuel Chan, Shirley Wong
and Marylois Chan

Exhibitions

1984	'London College of Furniture Show', London College of Furniture
1987	'Direct Design Show', The Royal Horticultural Halls, London
1987	'Middlesex University Degree Show', Chelsea Town Hall, London
1988	'New Art and Design', Fiell Gallery, New King's Road, London
1988	'The British Contemporary Furniture Show', The Royal Horticultural Halls, London
1989	'Sit '89', Business Design Centre, London
1990	'British Craftsmanship in Wood', Cheltenham College, Cheltenham
1993	'Interior Design International', Earl's Court, London
1995	'Celebration in British Craftsmanship', Cheltenham College, Cheltenham
1996-2010	'100% Design', Earl's Court, London
2001-2003	'International Contemporary Furniture Fair' (ICFF), Jacob K. Javits Convention Center, New York
2004	'Designed in the UK', Japantex, Tokyo
2010	*Wallpaper** Handmade', Salone del Mobile, Milan
2011	'designjunction', London Design Festival
2011	'designjunction', Salone del Mobile, Milan
2012	'designjunction', London Design Festival
2012	'designjunction', Salone del Mobile, Milan
2013	'designjunction', London Design Festival
2013	'New British', Vivienne Westwood flagship store, Salone del Mobile, Milan
2014	'Useful + Beautiful: Contemporary Design for the Home', Geffrye Museum, London
2014	'designjunction', London Design Festival
2015	'designjunction', London Design Festival
2015	'100% Design', Olympia, London
2015	'The Green Room', curated by designjunction, Salone del Mobile, Milan
2015	'House', Olympia, London
2016	*Wallpaper** Handmade', Salone del Mobile, Milan

Awards

2003	Flyt desk shortlisted in Furniture Design category, Design Week Awards, UK
2008	Classic Design Award (winner of Furniture Design category) for Hume book tower series, awarded by the Victoria & Albert Museum and *Homes & Gardens* magazine, UK
2009	Three Design Guild Marks for Motley drums, Motley bookcase and Motley dining table, The Furniture Makers' Company, UK (Samuel Chan was awarded three out of a total five Design Guild Marks given in 2009)
2010	Samuel Chan shortlisted in Best Designer category, British Design Awards, *ELLE Decoration*, UK
2010	Two Design Guild Marks for Motley baton chair and Motley pallet drawers, The Furniture Makers' Company, UK
2011	Perspective A&D Trophy (Product Design category) for Motley floor light, The Perspective Awards, Hong Kong
2011	Channels shortlisted in Best Design Brand category, British Design Awards, *ELLE Decoration*, UK
2011	Design Guild Mark for Gillespie side table, The Furniture Makers' Company, UK
2012	Perspective A&D Trophy (Furniture Design category) for Motley tall baton chair, The Perspective Awards, Hong Kong
2013	Two Design Guild Marks for Finnieston bookcase and Finnieston console, The Furniture Makers' Company, UK
2013	Perspective A&D Trophy (Lighting category) for Three Wise Men pendant lights, The Perspective Awards, Hong Kong
2014	Nomination for Furniture Designer category, *Homes & Gardens* Design Awards, UK
2014	Three Design Guild Marks for Joined + Jointed in its debut year: Concave bookcase (designed by Simon Pengelly), Jot desk (designed by Alex Hellum), Span dining table (designed by Wales & Wales), The Furniture Makers' Company, UK
2015	Furniture Designer of the Year, *Homes & Gardens* Design Awards, UK – judging panel commended Samuel for 'making wood sing'.
2015	Two Design Guild Marks for Kerning cabinet series and Kerning bookcase series, The Furniture Makers' Company, UK
2015	Perspective A&D Trophy (Furniture Design category) for Finnieston console, The Perspective Awards, Hong Kong
2016	Two Design Guild Marks for Column bookcases and Magnus chair, The Furniture Makers' Company, UK

Designs+ Projects

Curve chair

Design Year: 1987
Material: moulded beech-veneer plywood
Measurements: 73 x 36 x 43 cm
Manufacturer: self-production

'It was shown in the gallery of design historian Peter Fiell and bought by a Dutch furniture collector.'

As a youthful undergraduate, Samuel Chan designed this remarkable chair based on the Chinese character for 'girl'. Known as the Curve chair, for obvious reasons, it consists of four plywood elements all bent to exactly the same radius using a steam-moulding technique that relies on a considerable amount of heat and pressure. It is testament to Samuel's prodigious cabinetmaking ability that he was able to create such a technically complex yet simple-looking piece while still a student at Middlesex University. Ingeniously, Samuel designed the chair so that the four pieces of beech-faced plywood slotted together using hidden grooves, requiring only the minimum amount of glue to secure them together. The result was that the elements looked as though they were resting on one another rather than solidly joined, a fact that gave the design a remarkable visual lightness. As well as this one example, Samuel also created a version of the design in clear Perspex, which is still in his possession.

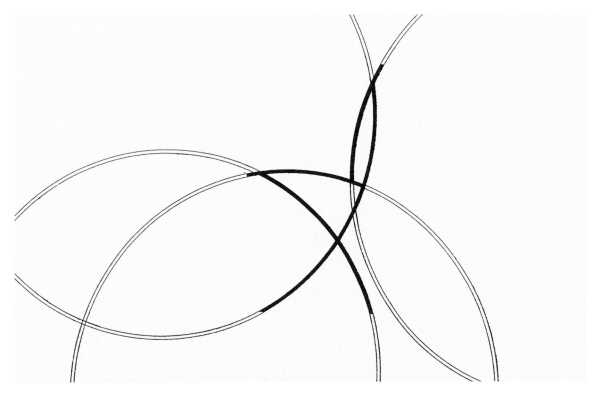

Alba high-backed chair

Design Year: 1988 (new edition: 1995)
Material: American white oak
Measurements: 100 x 45 x 45 cm
Manufacturer: self-production/Channels, London

While still a student at High Wycombe, Samuel became inspired not only by Japanese design, but also by the simple yet beautifully made furniture of the Shakers, whose motto was famously 'Hands to work, Hearts to God'. One of his first designs to reflect these influences was the Alba chair, with its distinctive high back and pared-down, minimalist aesthetic. Its name comes from the Latin binomial for white oak, *quercus alba* – the wood it was first executed in. It was originally designed as a dining chair as part of Samuel's MA final project, its execution first sponsored by the well-known timber merchant Albert Isherwood & Company. It was subsequently exhibited by the Fiell Gallery at 'Sit '89', together with a lower-backed lounge version and a matching bar stool. While the original design featured three small square-cut motifs in its back section, when Samuel reissued the chair as part of the Channels debut range in 1995, he decided to omit this detail and leave the back completely plain.

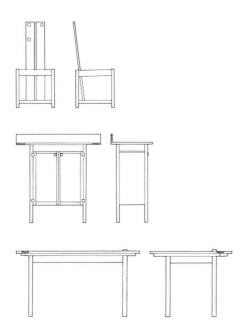

'I wanted to create pieces of furniture that express both contemporary design and classic woodcraft, and for that entire process – from concept to realization – to be seamless.'

Alba chest-of-seven-drawers

Design Year: 1995
Material: American white oak or American cherry
Measurements: 120 x 80 x 40 cm
Manufacturer: Channels, London

Samuel had begun using small, square cut-out motifs while studying furniture design at High Wycombe in the late 1980s. In 1996 he revived this detail in his design of the Alba chest-of-seven-drawers, but this time using it as a drawer pull. Over the years this simple yet functional clean-cut detail would become a signature Channels motif. In fact, the whole design of the Alba case piece was cleverly conceived as a play on squares. Using proportional measurements that were scrupulously worked out, Samuel was able to determine the exact size of the seven drawers – three square ones over four rectangular ones – and their spatial relationship not only to one another, but also to their cut-out drawer pulls, the broad overhanging top and the short back rail. Despite its refined proportions, this design was always intended to be a highly functional piece of furniture, for, as Samuel notes, 'I wanted it to retain the visual strength of the Alba style, but with a higher level of practicality.'

'With this design, Samuel lays down a strong statement of intent: proportion is a first principle in his design thinking.'

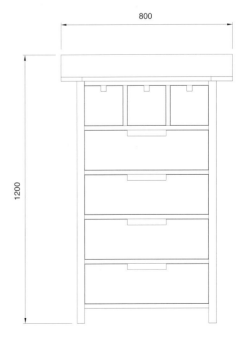

Memory Buffalo chair

Design Year: 1997
Material: American white oak or American cherry
Measurements: 80 x 64 x 74 cm
Manufacturer: Channels, London

In the late 1990s Samuel decided to explore his Chinese heritage, but within a contemporary furniture-making context. During this period, the only Chinese furniture available to purchase was either antique or reproduction, and he felt it was high time for a fresh approach. The resulting Memory collection was inspired by key pieces from the Ming period, yet when Samuel started studying these historic chairs he found that their proportions were 'all over the place'. He took it upon himself to rationalize those proportions in the design of his own modern, pared-down interpretation of the classic Chinese chair. The resulting Memory Buffalo chair, alongside the Monk chair from the same series, has a bold simplicity that echoes the past poignantly and, with its precisely executed and historically correct detailing – such as the curved buffalo-horn-shaped back rail that terminates in scrolling armrests – must also be appreciated for its extraordinary level of woodcraft.

'Clients who'd lived or worked in Asia found our contemporary pieces complemented the antique furniture they'd bought in the East.'

Memory CD cabinet

Design Year: 1997
Material: American white oak or American cherry
Measurements: 90 x 70 x 40 cm
Manufacturer: Channels, London

Although Chinese economic reform started under the leadership of Deng Xiaoping in the late 1970s, it was not until the 1990s that it really hit its stride, with large-scale privatization that set in place the right market conditions for China to become the economic powerhouse it is today. This 'opening up' of China, which had already begun in the 1980s, led to a great deal of interest in the West in Chinese culture, and so it is unsurprising that Samuel's Memory collection was received extremely well when it was launched in 1997, coincidentally the year of the 'handover' of Hong Kong from Britain to China. As its name suggests, this range intentionally evoked the forms and detailing of earlier Chinese furniture. One of the collection highlights is this cabinet, inspired by the multi-drawer chests used by practitioners of traditional Chinese medicine to store and categorize their herbs. Samuel's design was originally intended for the efficient storage of CDs, but could also be used just as well to store other small objects. In his approach, Samuel was not directly copying historic Chinese cabinets, but rather channelling their spirit in order to create a piece that was 'Chinese Modern' in essence.

'I find most Chinese furniture overly decorative, so I abandon carvings, use lighter timbers and adapt the function.'

Beka collection

Design Year: 1998
Materials: cherry, stainless steel
Measurements
Wardrobe: 180 x 88 x 66 cm
Dresser: 180 x 88 x 66 cm
Cabinet: 95 x 70 x 40 cm
Manufacturer: Channels, London

Although it had a strong Chinese flavour, this range of furniture, which included the elegant cabinets shown here, was markedly different from Samuel's earlier Memory series in that it did not reference any historic furniture antecedent. In contrast, Samuel took one iconic Chinese element – the round metal lock plate – simplified its form and updated it stylistically by making it from very contemporary satin-finished stainless steel. This made it, as he put it, 'a graphic rather than decorative detail'. This defining Chinese element of the collection was then incorporated into various clean-lined Western-style case pieces, some with matching stainless-steel frames. The resulting fusion designs demonstrated eloquently how skilfully Samuel was able to blend two very different cultural canons into eye-catching, hybrid pieces. While the collection captured a stylistic mood or attitude from the time, it nevertheless retains a timeless quality.

Wem collection

Design Year: 1999
Materials: American white oak or American black
walnut, stainless steel
Measurements
Sideboard I: 80 x 150 x 45 cm
Cabinet: 90 x 70 x 40 cm
Tallboy: 150 x 38 x 38 cm
Console table: 80 x 120 x 40 cm
Sideboard II: 80 x 150 x 40 cm

Named after Channels' Shropshire workshop in which
it is made, Wem was a landmark collection for Samuel
in that it came to define the Channels style: beautifully
made pieces with contemporary, clean lines. It has a
distinctive elemental simplicity that requires exacting
execution and precise detailing. For example, the Wem
dresser features perfectly book-matched panels of black
walnut, a shadow gap between its doors (eliminating
the need for pulls) and exposed stainless-steel hinges
set flush in its solid wood frame. The British Arts and
Crafts designer William Morris once famously observed
that 'Simplicity of life, even the barest, is not a misery,
but the very foundation of refinement,' and certainly
the Wem range accords with this sentiment, for
ultimately the 13 different pieces have an extraordinary
level of sophistication derived from Samuel's career-
long quest for aesthetic and functional simplicity. It
is now Channels' largest and one of its most popular
ranges. Samuel notes: 'After some time we were able
to identify the pieces that clients asked for all the
time, and so we began manufacturing some as stock
items in a choice of woods.' Undoubtedly, the enduring
popularity of the Wem collection is that its pieces are
not only functionally versatile, but also work very well
within different styles of interior.

'Simple designs are deceptive.
They only work if they are
superbly executed.'

Zac collection

Design Year: 2000
Material: English sycamore
Measurements
Four-poster bed: 210 x 162 x 208 cm
Work platform: 23 x 34/68 x 34 cm
Manufacturer: Channels, London

One of Samuel's favourite woods is English sycamore, a pale, almost white timber with a very fine, even grain. For his Zac collection, he wanted to create a range of furniture that was almost ethereally light, and so sycamore was the obvious choice of wood. Comprising a simple four-poster bed, a mirror and a clothes rack, the collection was also the first that Samuel conceptualized around a narrative based on the person for whom he was designing the pieces. Samuel wanted to create 'a dream-like room' for an imaginary man called Zac, who was highly cerebral and 'liked to do most of his thinking in bed'. Samuel found this type of 'method designing' extremely helpful, and has since used it a number of times in planning his collections. By creating a fictional character, he finds he can focus on the needs and desires of a very specific type of client. When the Zac collection was launched, in 2000, it received a large amount of press attention thanks to its Zen-inspired minimalism, which gave the pieces a wonderfully airy lightness. The collection encapsulated the millennial tendency for predominantly modern, clean-lined, uncluttered, minimal interiors, which were in many ways a reaction against the postmodern excesses of the 1980s and early 1990s.

Juxa collection

Design Year: 2001
Materials: oak
Measurements
Secretaire: 156 x 170 x 57 cm
Lounger: 70 x 140 x 70 cm
Manufacturer: Channels, London

Samuel has always enjoyed observing and reflecting upon changing cultural attitudes, and in the early 2000s he noticed that many of his private clients wanted spaces in which they could work from home, but that did not have the look of a traditional office. The Juxa collection was all about creating an idealized space that skilfully juxtaposed work and play, with one end of a room dedicated to work and the other to more leisurely pursuits. For the work zone, Samuel created a purpose-built secretaire, a high-backed armchair and a leather-topped table, while for the 'chill-out' area he designed a matching lounger, table, hat stand and bar. Extremely simple in its design, yet exquisitely crafted, Juxa was distinguished from the Wem collection by the use of heavier panels and larger offset supporting frames. As Marylois notes, the secretaire was designed as 'a sort of secret indulgence', for although it is beautifully fitted out inside with different-sized leather-fronted drawers and slide-out shelves, when its pocket doors are closed no one can see the bespoke craftsmanship that lies within.

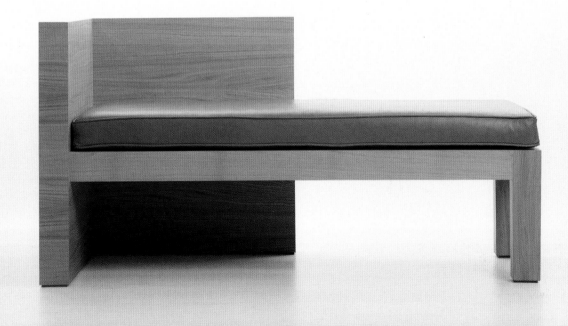

The Trafalgar

Design Year: 2001
Location: Trafalgar Square, London
Client: Hilton Hotels & Resorts

Since 2000, Channels' activity in the hotel furniture market has grown significantly thanks to the comprehensive 'design to installation' service it provides. The Trafalgar, just off London's bustling Trafalgar Square, was a very important hotel project for Channels, being the first major commission for which it performed the role of both designer and manufacturer of the specified furniture. It marked a milestone for the client, too, being Hilton's first foray into what it then described as 'lifestyle' hotels. Samuel's design for the project drew on his existing Wem collection, made unique through the inclusion of many bespoke elements. With its clean, contemporary look and award-winning Rockwell Bar, the hotel exuded contemporary luxury, but without any of the clubby fussiness that has been associated with so many landmark hotels in the past.

Flyt collection

Design Year: 2002
Material: American white oak or American black walnut
Measurements
Square cabinet: 115 x 112 x 45 cm
Low unit: 40 x 196 x 50 cm
Writing desk: 77 x 180 x 80 cm
Manufacturer: Channels, London

'We called this collection Flyt because it is all about lightness.'

The Flyt writing desk and dressing table, according to Mike France of the Wem workshop, are some of Channels' most technically challenging pieces to make, because their extremely thin tops – just 10 mm thick – and finger-joint detail require a huge amount of cabinetmaking know-how to get precisely right. Likewise, their beautiful top-mounted drawers and the foldaway mirror element take great skill to execute to Samuel's exacting standards; the manufacture must be precise to the millimetre. The Flyt collection also includes a two- or four-door square cabinet and a low unit, both of which are extremely minimal in their design, with a pared-down, elemental quality that gives them a certain visual lightness. The name of the range refers to Samuel's desire to create a furniture family with a much airier aesthetic than his previous designs. In fact, the Flyt collection would came to epitomize Samuel's reductionist approach to design during the early 2000s. The Flyt desk was shortlisted for the Design Week Awards in 2003, and its inclusion highlighted the beginning of a revived interest in the role of craft in contemporary design.

Flyt chair + Toro chair

Design Year: 2002
Materials
Flyt chair: moulded wood-veneer plywood, American white oak or American black walnut
Toro chair: American white oak or American black walnut, leather
Measurements
Flyt chair: 79 x 42 x 42 cm
Toro chair: 77 x 56 x 50 cm
Manufacturer: Channels, London

'It is always the experimenting that motivates Sam creatively.'

In 2002, while Samuel was designing the Flyt collection, he decided to explore the idea of creating a new chair that could be produced in volume. He came up with two designs, the Flyt chair and the Toro chair, both of which are distinguished by their very compact proportions. The ergonomic wood-veneered moulded plywood seating section of the Flyt chair was inspired by a number of mid-century designs – including Charles and Ray Eames's Plywood Group – and speculated on the potential of high-volume production. Yet, rather than using a metal base as with many plywood-seat shell chairs, Samuel decided on a simple, solid wood base. By contrasting the shapely curves of the plywood with the rigid geometry of the chair's supporting structure, he was able to create a simply constructed design with a very strong Japanese flavour. For the Toro chair, on the other hand, Samuel took an archetypal bull-horn chair form that he has always liked and simplified it into an elemental design with exquisite, ideal proportions, much as the Danish designer Hans Wegner did with his own bull-horn chairs in the early 1950s. As with so much of Samuel's work, when one contemplates the carefully chamfered back rail of the Toro chair one is reminded of Ludwig Mies van der Rohe's famous aphorism: 'God is in the details.'

Lamb Chambers

Design Year: 2003
Location: Middle Temple, London
Client: Lamb Chambers

Founded by a number of eminent legal practitioners, Lamb Chambers is a leading firm of barristers who specialize in civil-dispute resolution and litigation. Situated in London's legal heartland, known as the Temple, and close to the Royal Courts of Justice, Lamb Chambers underwent a major interior renovation in 2003. As part of this refurbishment programme the chamber's four-room arbitration suite was refurnished by Channels using pieces from its extensive Wem collection, as well as other bespoke yet matching pieces designed specially for the project. In common with most of Samuel's early pieces, the furniture made for Lamb Chambers was executed in American cherry. This North American close-grain hardwood is valued for the warmth of its beautiful reddish, almost honey-coloured hue.

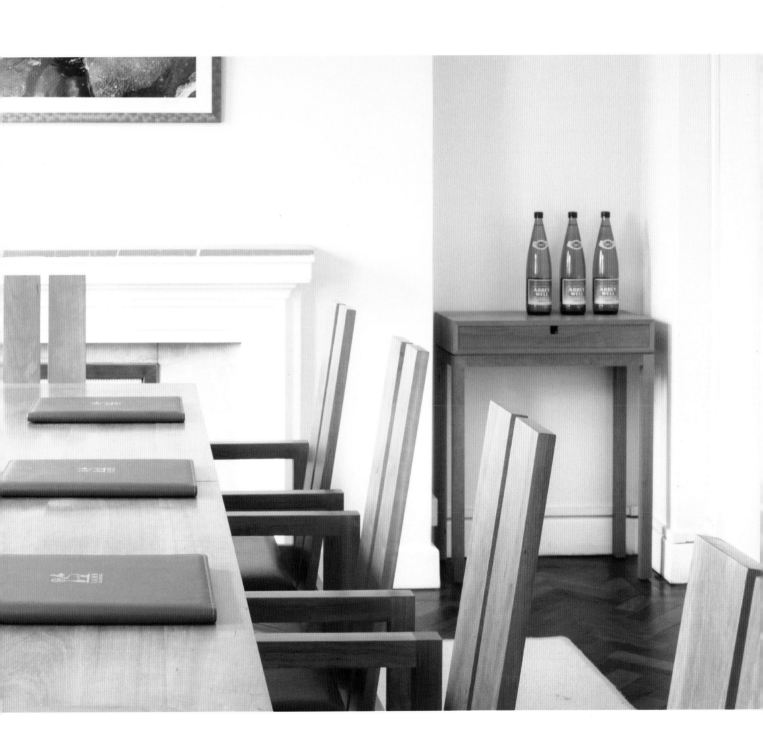

Tot collection

Design Year: 2003
Material: American white oak or American black walnut
Measurements
Chair: 61 x 39 x 32 cm
Toy-box: 46 x 80 x 40 cm
Manufacturer: Channels, London

The Tot collection came about because many of Samuel's clients, unable to find children's furniture in keeping with their interior schemes, asked him whether he could come up with anything suitable. In fact, in the early 2000s much of the children's furniture available was either traditional or garishly cartoonish. By contrast, Samuel decided that any children's collection must focus on function and design longevity, so that children could not only use the pieces easily, but also grow up with them. He therefore designed a cabinet that split in half to form two low units – one with drawers and the other with a hanging rail – so that when a child was young the pieces would be the right height, but as he or she grew older the two could be stacked to form a higher single unit with shelves replacing the hanging rail. Samuel also intended his Tot toy-box to be used beyond childhood, being adaptable as a coffee table or storage chest when the child grew up. With no sharp edges and generous cut-out pulls, the Tot collection was designed specifically for children to use safely and easily, yet its functional versatility and simple pared-down aesthetics meant that it was not in any way 'childish'. The Tot collection also includes a mini version of Samuel's Flyt chair, which – despite its refined appearance – is impressively robust yet light enough for a child to move alone.

Samuel and his son, Jasper,
with the Tot collection, 2003

63

Accessories range

Design Year: 2003
Material: American white oak or American black walnut
Measurements
CD/DVD stand: 175 x 45 x 80 cm
Square tray: 4 x 40 x 40 cm
Desktop accessories: various dimensions
Manufacturer: Channels, London

Over the years, Samuel had sourced accessories from various European design houses to 'dress' his furniture in Channels' showroom on New King's Road. In 2003, however, he decided to try his hand at designing his own range of accessories. Using oak and walnut, he created various desktop pieces, as well as storage boxes of different sizes, two trays, a paper bin, a candlestick and a vase. New oak and walnut versions of Samuel's

wall-leaning CD/DVD stand (previously designed in 1998) were also launched in 2003 as part of this new collection. Simple but beautifully crafted in solid timber, this range of designs with its exposed finger-joint detail recalls the strong functional purity of earlier Shaker designs. Quite simply, these pieces are both useful and beautiful thanks in no small part to the fact that their forms follow their functions.

COCM Centre

Design Year: 2003
Location: Padstow Avenue, Milton Keynes
Client: Chinese Overseas Christian Mission

In 1948 the pastor Stephen Wang, who was then headmaster of one of the largest Methodist schools in China, took a year's sabbatical in order to study at Cambridge University. While he was there the Communists seized power in his homeland and he found himself effectively exiled, for his associations with the West would have undoubtedly prompted a warrant for his arrest were he to return. While pondering his situation, he realized that Chinese people living in Europe had no one to lead them to Christianity, and he felt that it was God's will that he become an evangelist. With this aim, Wang founded the Chinese Overseas Christian Mission (COCM) in 1950 in order to bring the gospel not only to Chinese people living in Europe, but also to 'local' Europeans. The Mission originally operated from a Victorian house in London, but grew to such an extent over the decades that in 2003 it decided to move to a much larger, purpose-built centre in leafy Milton Keynes. Samuel was asked to furnish the building's light-filled contemporary spaces, from its dining and conference areas to its bedrooms and finely appointed library. Much of the furniture was designed specifically for the project, including a custom leather-upholstered version of Samuel's Flyt chair, helping to tie the different rooms together visually and give the project a strong sense of design continuity.

PUBLIC

Design Year: 2003
Location: Elizabeth Street, Nolita, New York City
Client: AvroKO Group

For their design of PUBLIC restaurant in New York City, AvroKO – a leading architecture and interior design consultancy with a reputation for creating off-beat, forward-looking, concept-driven spaces for the hospitality sector – decided to take as their design theme mid-century public buildings, as the name of the eatery suggests. Incorporating salvaged 'industrial' pieces, such as filing-card cabinets, post-office boxes and an old office clock, the scheme also featured a bespoke version of Samuel's very contemporary plywood-backed Flyt chair, which was fitted with a slim leather seat pad to provide greater comfort for diners. The contrast of old and new proved to be a winning formula: AvroKO was subsequently given a James Beard Outstanding Restaurant Design award for the interior scheme of this very stylish restaurant. Today, PUBLIC remains a popular Michelin-starred New York institution, while the flanking rows of Flyt chairs still look great in the very chic industrial-themed space.

Kong Fok Church

Design Year: 2004
Location: Harcourt Road, Hong Kong Island
Client: Kong Fok Church

After years of conducting its weekly Sunday services in a hired hotel ballroom, Kong Fok Church eventually took over the entire floor of a building in the heart of Hong Kong's thriving business district. Effectively starting with a blank slate, Samuel was asked to furnish the new church with designs that reflected 'the familiar atmosphere of a traditional place of worship but with a contemporary aesthetic'. Using American oak, Samuel designed a simple but substantial pew system, as well as a pulpit, a communion table, a central cross and flanking screens. The overall effect of the minimal design is of a light-filled transcendental space that is spiritually far removed from the bustling streets surrounding it.

Voyage collection

Design Year: 2004
Material: American black walnut
Measurements
Chair: 79 x 42 x 42 cm
Desk: 77 x 180 x 55 cm
Diversion station: 130 x 70 x 40 cm
Manufacturer: Channels, London

The Voyage collection reflected, as Marylois explains, 'where we were in 2004, when Samuel was starting to do a lot of hotel projects'. As a consequence, he began thinking about the kind of experience a traveller might want from a hotel. With its contemporary minimalist-craft fusion aesthetic, the Voyage collection was conceived first and foremost as a 'brand-free' room set, comprising just a bed, a chair, a desk and a 'diversion station'. These four key pieces, constituting all anyone needed when away from home, were consciously created to have none of the aesthetic constraints that are generally associated with hotel brands. Samuel also wanted to create a sense of airiness and lightness, so to make the desk he employed an extremely thin (10 mm) top resting on two open-framework pedestals. Yet despite its minimal aesthetic, this piece was sophisticated in its detailing, especially where the top was angled downwards at 90 degrees to the sides to form a lip-like element. Likewise, the Voyage diversion station was designed to be as compact and mobile as possible, for, as Samuel explains, flat-screen televisions 'were becoming a standard feature in both our residential and hotel projects, but the idea of fixing them permanently to a wall when these TVs are supposed to be about greater flexibility and freedom was – for me – a contradiction'. Sitting on castors and a swivelling mechanism, the diversion station could be angled easily for optimum viewing, enabling the user to watch their favourite programmes not only from the comfort of the chair, but also from the bed.

The Tea Gallery

Design Year: 2005
Location: Allen Street, New York City
Client: The Tea Gallery

Michael Wong and his father ran an Asian antiques business in downtown Manhattan for many years, and in the Chinese tradition always offered cups of tea to visiting customers. Over time many of their clients became curious about the different types of tea being served and the techniques being used to brew them, so much so that in 2000 Michael and his wife, Winnie, decided to transform the antiques shop into a dedicated tea gallery. In 2005 the couple, who share a great passion for tea, commissioned Samuel to transform the shop into a thoroughly contemporary gallery space that could be used for formal tea ceremonies as well as providing a beautiful setting for Michael's extensive collection of teapots. Incorporating various 'stock' pieces from Channels, as well as a number of pieces designed specially by Samuel, the gallery had a very sophisticated Chinese Modern look. In fact, the Wongs were so pleased with Samuel's work that their gallery became a de facto Channels showroom, eventually stocking a wide range of his furniture and accessories.

Tenth Anniversary collection

Design Year: 2005
Material: zebrano
Measurements: various
Manufacturer: Channels, London

In 2005, to commemorate Channels' first decade in business, Samuel created a very special anniversary collection, comprising ten significant 'signature' designs executed in zebrano. This distinctive stripy timber – also known as zebrawood, for obvious reasons – is an exotic hardwood that comes mainly from central Africa and features wide bands of golden sapwood interspersed with narrow dark-brown streaks. An extremely heavy and hard timber with a rippling grain, it was difficult to work with, but the results were more than worth the effort, giving these limited-edition 'birthday' pieces a very special, luxurious quality.

Daio dining table and chairs

Design Year: 2005
Material: American white oak
Measurements
Dining chair: 73 x 50 x 61 cm
Table: 63 cm x 170 cm (dia.)
Manufacturer: Channels, London

Designed in Channels' tenth anniversary year, the Daio collection takes a cultural cue from the Far East: the dining table with matching chairs is set at a much lower height than is traditionally found in the West. This lowered sitting position allows a much more intimate and relaxed dining experience, much as one finds in Japanese homes, where the use of short-legged tables known as *chabudai* is commonplace. Launched at the '100% Design' show in London in 2005, the Daio collection reflected a new stylistic direction for Channels, featuring for the first time the use of a contrasting colour alongside the natural oak in the complementary cabinets. In many ways, the Daio chair was a refinement of Samuel's earlier Toro chair, for it also featured a beautifully chamfered bull-horn-shaped back rail. Samuel prefers an evolutionary step-by-step approach to design, and will often hone a particular element across a number of designs and over a period of several years.

Hume collection

Design Year: 2006
Material: American white oak
Measurements
Low: 50 x 50 x 50 cm
Medium: 100 x 45 x 45 cm
Tall: 115 x 112 x 45 cm
Manufacturer: Channels, London, and Channels for Linteloo, Zeist, the Netherlands

The Hume book towers are contemporary interpretations of the two-tier revolving bookcases that were so popular during the Victorian and Edwardian eras. Unlike their elaborate predecessors, however, these designs are stripped down and have an architectural quality. They were named by Samuel's wife, Shirley, as a tribute to the eighteenth-century Scottish philosopher, historian, economist and essayist David Hume, who wrote a number of major philosophical works, most notably *A Treatise of Human Nature* (1739–40) and *Enquiry Concerning the Principles of Morals* (1751). Hume was also librarian for the Edinburgh Faculty of Advocates – and that is why his name was chosen for these library-themed pieces. As well as providing compact shelving space for books, these four-sided rotating towers can accommodate CDs and other objects. In 2007 the Hume book towers won the Classic Design Award from the Victoria and Albert Museum and *Homes & Gardens* magazine, a fitting tribute to a design that looks to the past but is also very much of its own time.

Malmaison Oxford

Design Year: 2006
Location: Oxford Castle complex, Oxford
Client: Malmaison & Hotel du Vin Group

In 2006 Channels was asked by the Malmaison hotel group to design and make furniture for a new hotel in Oxford. The project, in a former jail within the historic precincts of Oxford Castle, was an unusual one and needed very skilful handling. Behind the imposing facade of this Victorian prison, the cells themselves were turned into guest rooms that retained their original barred windows and reinforced iron doors. In tribute to the 'dark drama' of the building, Samuel created a furniture scheme with strong lines and an impressive scale, but at the same time a contemporary, luxurious feel. The furniture was significantly heavier both in weight and in style than is normal among Samuel's creations, and yet it was perfectly pitched given the unique context. More than anything, the project showed how responsive Samuel can be to a very specific brief, and the way he can engender a special sense of place through his furniture designs.

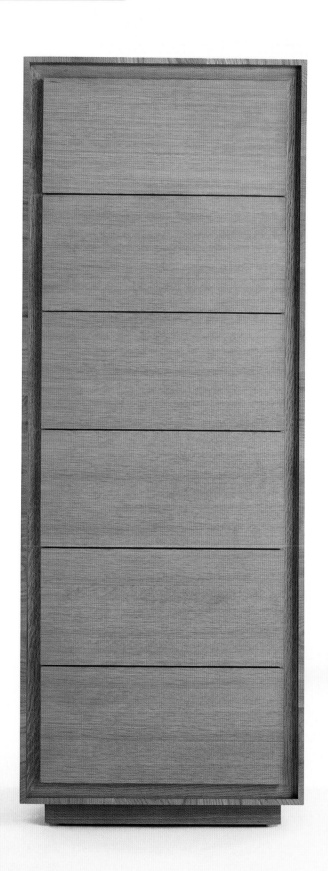

Motley I cabinets

Design Year: 2007
Material: natural oak or smoked oak
Measurements
Tallboy: 130 x 50 x 50 cm
Low unit: 27 x 180 x 60 cm
Manufacturer: Channels, London

'This deceptively simple cabinet collection has a wealth of detail.'

One of Samuel's favourite anecdotes about Mike France, the manager of the Channels workshop, recalls the time Mike phoned Samuel in the studio to ask about one of his drawings: 'You've specified two metres, but I can only give you 1,998 millimetres – is that alright?' Mike proceeded to explain why that was the case, while Samuel chuckled over his cabinetmaker's genuine concern over the loss of 2 millimetres: 'I might laugh about it, but it's that attitude that makes Mike France invaluable.' Over the years, Samuel has come to rely on Mike's ability to turn out pieces that have an innate visual simplicity but are in fact complicated to achieve. This versatile, functional collection of Motley cabinets is a good example. Not only have their harmonious proportions been worked out thoroughly so that they are perfect to the nearest millimetre, but also the detailing of each piece has been considered carefully and then executed exquisitely. For instance, the pieces' outer frames are edged with solid wood lippings that are applied painstakingly by hand, while the recessed borders around each drawer make them stand out elegantly in relief. The pieces are also raised on short plinth-like pedestals for greater presence and grace. It is these quiet details – and the meticulous craft that goes into achieving them – that elevate the designs from the simple to the simply beautiful.

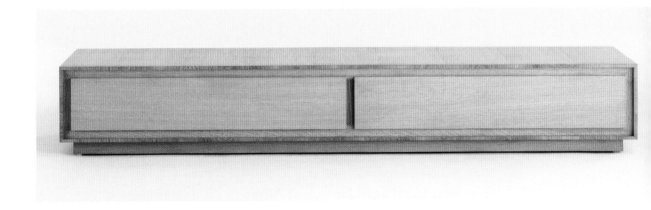

Motley I birch drums

Design Year: 2007
Material: Scandinavian birch plywood
Measurements
Short: 42 cm x 40 cm (dia.)
Tall: 67 cm x 40 cm (dia.)
Small: 35 cm x 60 cm (dia.)
Large: 35 cm x 80 cm (dia.)
Manufacturer: Channels, London, and Channels for
Wildspirit, Knokke-Heist, Belgium

In 2007 Channels acquired new equipment that enabled it to 'do more curves'. Around this time, Samuel had also come into contact with a new supplier of Scandinavian birch plywood and so began experimenting with large blocks of plywood using his brand-new tools. The results were four drum-like forms that could be used either as stools or as small occasional tables. Like the Finnish designer Tapio Wirkkala, who famously sculpted leaf-shaped platters from teak and birch plywood, Samuel exploited the material's beautiful laminated striations, which bring to mind the annual rings of a tree. While experimenting with the plywood blocks, Samuel found that the material lent itself to a more sculptural handling than did the solid woods and veneers with which he had previously worked, and he revelled in being able to explore a more free-flowing vocabulary of form.

'As a child, I was always curious about how objects were put together. I also wanted to invent things.'

Motley II benches

Design Year: 2007
Material: American white oak
Measurements
Small: 34/50 x 75 x 28 cm
Medium: 34/50 x 100 x 28 cm
Large: 34/50 x 150 x 28 cm
Manufacturer: Channels, London

In times gone by, wooden benches were a common feature in domestic settings: it was only people of high status who could afford chairs, and lesser mortals had to make do with sitting on simply jointed stools and benches. Indeed, the term 'chairman' reflects this historic association of the chair with high status. During the twentieth century, however, the traditional bench became less popular than in previous centuries, especially in the home, presumably because of its utilitarian connotations. Yet the humble jointed wooden bench is in fact a very practical and durable piece of furniture, and Samuel was drawn not only to its constructional simplicity, but also to its functional honesty. Revisiting this historic furniture type, Samuel's Motley benches come in three sizes and are made with solid oak frames that are fixed with beautifully cut traditional tenon joints, detailed to be visible on the seat itself. In many ways these simple yet robust designs accord with William Morris's desire to create 'good citizen's furniture' – which was always the aim of the Arts and Crafts movement, and is still Samuel's goal.

'Exposed tenon joints create four square motifs, highlighting the woodworking detail.'

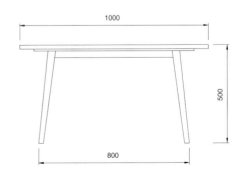

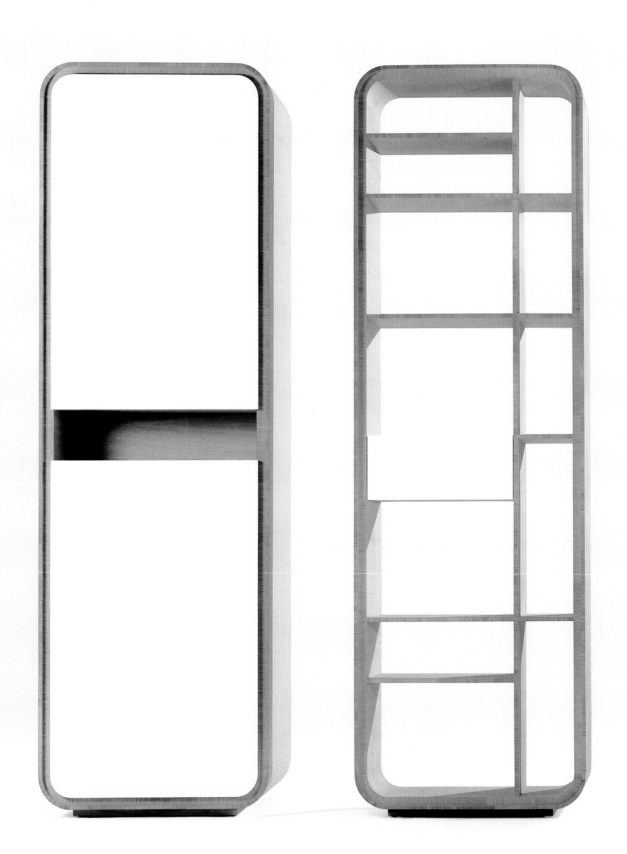

Motley II wardrobe, bookcase + sideboard

Design Year: 2008
Materials: American white oak, white matte lacquer
Measurements
Wardrobe: 220 x 70 x 60 cm
Bookcase: 220 x 70 x 40 cm
Sideboard: 72 x 220 x 50 cm
Manufacturer: Channels, London

With their rounded contours, the Motley II bookcase, wardrobe and sideboard reflected the softer-edged look of the late 2000s, as well as a growing sculptural confidence within Samuel's own work. The initial inspiration came from a photo of a door that Samuel found while leafing through a journal: 'The door had rounded corners, and that caught my attention. I was also fascinated by the door frame - which was of course rounded as well - and how precisely the door fitted into it.' Although it introduced a new shape, the Motley II collection shows continuity with the earlier Motley cabinets in the recessed border detail that frames the main panels. Executed in oak with a contrasting matte white lacquer, they still relied heavily on superlative craftsmanship; in fact, the edges hand-finished with cross-grain solid wood lippings were even harder to achieve on the curves. Motley II signalled a departure both at the drawing board and the workbench, and was a success: the bookcase from the collection was lauded with a Design Guild Mark in 2009, an award established by the Furniture Makers' Company to recognize and reward excellence among British designers creating furniture for volume production.

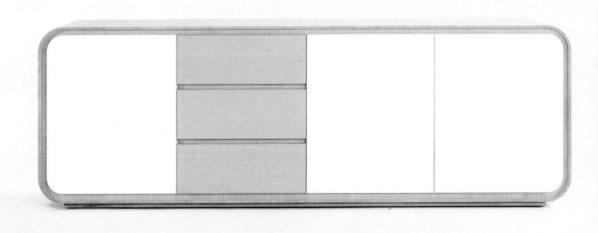

Motley II dining table + coffee table

Design Year: 2008
Materials: Corian®, American white oak
Measurements
Dining table: 74 x 220 x 120 cm
Coffee table: 40 x 99 x 54 cm
Manufacturer: Channels, London

Founded in 1802, the Du Pont company is well known for creating groundbreaking chemicals and innovative plastics, and one of its most famous branded materials is Corian, a composite of acrylic polymer and alumina trihydrate developed by the company's scientists in 1967. Originally produced as a material for countertops, during the early twenty-first century Corian was actively promoted by Du Pont to the international design community, through the sponsorship of various exhibitions and initiatives. This ultimately led more designers to explore its inherent physical properties and incorporate it into their designs. In 2008, as part of his new exploration into rounded forms, Samuel created the Motley II dining table and coffee table, his first designs to combine Corian with solid wood. It was a perfect match of the man-made and the natural; Channels' cabinetmakers worked the Corian like a piece of wood, and its chalky white surfaces emphasized the natural grain of the solid oak. Not surprisingly, this skilful combination of old and new was widely praised by the design press, and earned Samuel his second British Design Guild Mark in 2009.

'A design that combines timeless woodcraft with contemporary materials.'

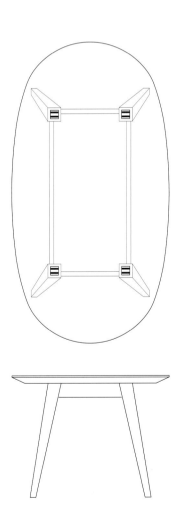

Motley II baton drums + cedar drums

Design Year: 2008
Material: reclaimed Canadian cedar or solid oak
Measurements
Short: 42 cm x 40 cm (dia.)
Tall: 67 cm x 40 cm (dia.)
Small: 35 cm x 60 cm (dia.)
Large: 35 cm x 80 cm (dia.)
Manufacturer: Channels, London; and Channels for Wildspirit, Knokke-Heist, Belgium, and Channels for Mossi, Tiel, the Netherlands

As we have seen, Samuel designed his first 'drums' using blocks of birch plywood in 2007. The following year, however, he decided to adapt the designs by using sections of reclaimed Canadian cedar, which meant these pieces could now be used both indoors and outdoors (the birch versions having only been suitable for use inside). These 'revisited' designs are cut from wooden blocks made of 12-mm-thick sheets of finger-joined cedar pieces laminated together. Ingeniously functioning as both seats and tables, each drum has its own unique wood pattern that is intrinsic to its manufacture. Innovative in form, function, materials and technique, the cedar drums from the Motley II collection were also given a Design Guild Mark, which brought Channels' tally in 2009 to three or, as the Furniture Makers' Company announced, 'a hat-trick for Samuel Chan'. In the same year, Samuel made another variant of the drums using hand-cut batons of oak. These ribbed drums were not only visually and materially lighter, but also possessed a more Oriental feeling, reminding one of traditional Chinese birdcages. The Dutch design company Mossi also sold special versions of Samuel's baton drums in natural and dark brown oak under the name Bubo Bubo.

Motley II Pebble tables + stools

Design Year: 2008
Material: American white oak or American white oak, leather
Measurements
Small table: 40 x 31 x 39 cm
Medium table: 52 x 35 x 47 cm
Large table: 65 x 46 x 57 cm
Stool: 42 x 30 x 36 cm
Manufacturer: Channels, London

The Motley II collection, in common with the Motley I range from the previous year, was designed using new technical processes that enabled Samuel to create forms with a far more organic quality than his previous work, which was typified by a strong geometric linearity. The Pebble tables were a perfect example of this new sculptural direction with their free-form asymmetrical tops of solid white oak on tapering wooden legs. Intended as side or coffee tables, these designs, each with a slightly differently shaped top, look especially good when clustered as a trio, like pebbles on a beach. The Pebble stools from the same collection were crafted using various shades of grey leather on the seat for a softer finish.

Booktower

Design Year: 2008
Material: matt-black-finish oak
Measurements
Version I: 150 x 45 x 45 cm
Version II: 100 x 45 x 45 cm
Version III: 49 x 49 x 49 cm
Version XXL: 184 x 79 x 79 cm
Manufacturer: Channels, London, for Linteloo, Zeist,
The Netherlands

As well as creating his own designs for Channels and Joined + Jointed, Sam also occasionally designs for other companies. Having established a very good manufacturing relationship with the Dutch furniture company Linteloo, he was asked in 2008 by its founder, Jan te Lintelo, to create special matt-black versions of his Hume bookcases for the Zeist-based company. Sam also designed for Linteloo a towering 'XXL' version of the largest bookcase, which – at more than 1.8 metres tall – has a commanding presence in any room while also providing useful storage for any number of things. Linteloo notes: 'Any book will find a home in this practical design by Samuel Chan, whether it is standing up or lying down. But also a vase or a precious object will feel right at home in this multifunctional "tower".' Interestingly, when executed in a matt-black finish, this design reminds one of the geometric abstraction beloved by members of the Dutch De Stijl movement, including Gerrit Rietveld, who famously designed the iconic Red/Blue chair in 1918/23 – which is probably why Jan te Lintelo was so attracted to Chan's pieces in the first place. It is not by chance that Sam's Booktower channels the spirit of De Stijl, for as a student he was fascinated by the formal purity of Rietveld's work. Indeed, the early crate-like sideboard he designed for the Albert Isherwood project was in many ways a tribute to Rietveld's earlier case furniture pieces with their strong rectilinear forms.

'Purity of line, proportion and superb craftsmanship are the trademarks of Samuel's work.'

Sarah Stewart Smith, Telegraph *magazine*

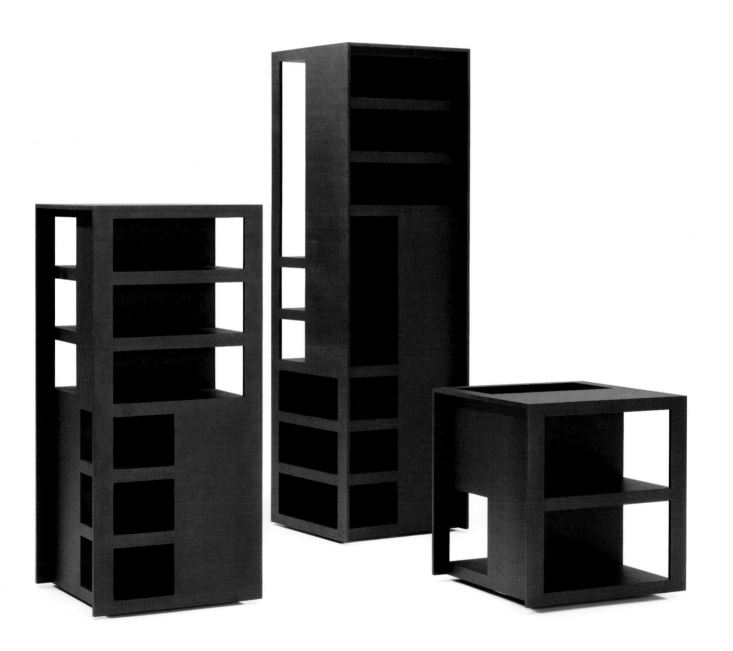

Motley III baton drum chair

Design Year: 2009
Materials: white oak, wool felt
Measurements (per unit): 74 cm x 80 cm (dia.)
Manufacturer: Channels, London

Left: Motley III baton drum
chairs in the lobby of the
Jumeirah Himalayas Hotel in
Shanghai

Having explored the constructional possibilities of wooden batons in his design for the Motley II drums in 2008, the following year Samuel created a round armchair similarly constructed from hand-carved sections of solid oak. Set on a low revolving base, this tub chair with its supporting cage of wooden struts had a strong Oriental identity, and can best be described as within the Chinese Modern style, which Samuel is defining better perhaps than any other designer working at the moment. With its scooped seat upholstered in wool felt, a favourite Channels covering material, this chair has a wonderful textural quality, and the two natural materials – oak and wool – complement each other beautifully. The judges for the Furniture Makers' Company Design Guild Marks must have thought so, too: the Motley III baton drum chair won this acclaimed furniture design award in 2010.

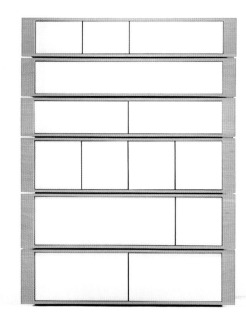

Motley III pallet drawer + shelving systems

Design Year: 2009
Materials: American white oak, white matte lacquer
Measurements (per unit): 15/21 x 83 x 50 cm
Manufacturer: Channels, London

One of the founding ambitions of Channels was to offer bespoke design - a service that is quite rare in contemporary furniture design. Samuel explains, 'The bespoke element is very important to me. I love the idea of the customer being involved in creating a piece of furniture from the start. It assures them that their piece is truly one-of-a-kind, and they develop an emotional connection to it even while it's being made.' As he reflected on how to make his bespoke service more distinctive, Samuel started working on how to make furniture 'customizable' in other ways. The Motley pallet drawer and shelving system is his way of offering 'instant and long-term bespoke options' to the user. He came up with six different drawer designs - each one stands alone as a single 'pallet': 'If the client wants a low side cabinet, they can buy just three pallets. Or they can buy more and play around with how to arrange them. The pallets slot neatly on top of each other without any fixings, so you can change the configuration easily, and add to it over time.' While the inspiration for the form and functionality of the design comes from the humble wooden loading pallet, Samuel's version is painstakingly detailed with recessed drawer fronts on push-catches. The sides are also recessed for easy handling, and the entire frame finished with hand-applied solid wood lippings, cut across the grain to provide a subtle but strong visual emphasis. The Motley III pallet shelving system is similarly conceived as a modular design. The innovative drawer system was awarded a Design Guild Mark in 2010.

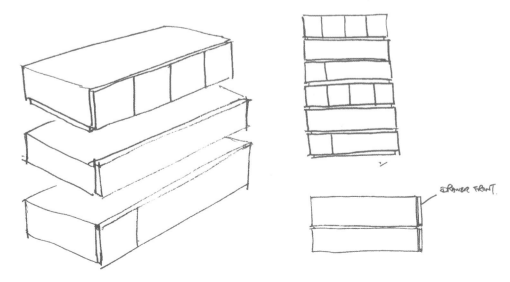

Motley lamps

Design Year: 2009
Materials: white or smoked oak-veneer plywood,
American white oak or smoked oak, frosted glass
Measurements
Large floor lamp: 200 cm x 80 cm (dia.)
Medium floor lamp: 170 cm x 60 cm (dia.)
Small floor lamp: 120 cm x 50 cm (dia.)
Manufacturer: Channels, London, and Channels for
Mossi, Tiel, the Netherlands

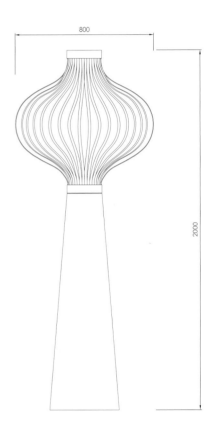

The Motley floor lamps and pendant lights are among
Samuel's most iconic designs to date, bringing a touch
of Oriental warmth to any room with their distinctive
lantern-like shades in natural or smoked oak. However,
Samuel notes, 'I didn't so much have Chinese lanterns
in mind as the paper lanterns that children make by
cutting slits in a single piece of paper.' A frosted-glass
cylinder held within each lantern shade helps to diffuse
the beams emitted from the hidden light source, while
the hand-cut plywood ribs of the lanterns scatter this
softened light in a very evocative manner. The pendant
lights have the same lantern elements as the floor
models, but are suspended from the ceiling instead of
resting on matching trunk-like solid-wood bases. Both
types are available in three sizes.

The Dutch design company Mossi also sold these
designs, under the name Otus. These highly distinctive
lights exude a 'memories of China' aesthetic, which
was especially suited to the public spaces of the
Jumeirah Himalayas Hotel, a design-and-make
furnishing project that Samuel undertook in 2011.
In the same year, the Motley lamp was a winner
in the product design category of The Perspective
Architecture & Design Trophy Awards, one of Asia
Pacific's foremost design accolades.

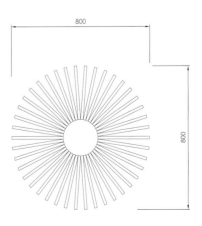

Egg chairs

Design Year: 2009
Material: ash
Measurements: 56 x 90 x 60 cm
Manufacturer: Channels, London

Samuel explains: 'I made these 'egg' chairs from ash
wood with a lathe and chisel. Before I start carving, I
ask: what can a piece of wood do? I then work out the
ergonomics and go with the flow. I don't use colour,
because I like the wood to express its own distinctive
beauty.' Functioning more as stools than as chairs,
although technically the latter, these sculpted wooden
seats capture the abstract essence of nature and have
a strong presence, much like the artworks of Henry
Moore or Barbara Hepworth. Made from blocks of
laminated ash, the chairs have layered striations that
accentuate the natural grain of the various wooden
pieces, giving the designs an attractive yet understated
decorative interest.

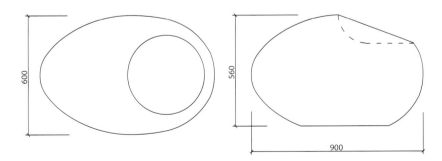

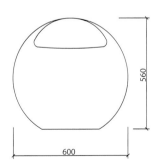

Motley tall baton chair

Design Year: 2010
Materials: American white oak, wool felt
Measurements: 140 cm x 90 cm (dia.)
Manufacturer: Channels, London

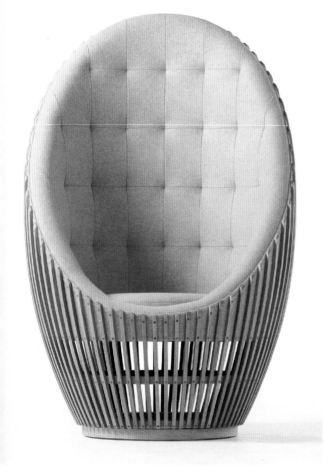

In common with many Scandinavian designers, both past and present, Samuel believes in an evolutionary approach to design, whereby certain forms are honed functionally and aesthetically over various designs and across a period of years. The Motley tall baton chair, for instance, is an evolution of the Motley baton drum chair (2009), which is itself an evolution of the Motley baton drums (2008). Indeed, this unusual and inventive wooden 'baton' construction has become something of a Channels leitmotif. The Motley tall baton chair is, however, far bolder stylistically than its predecessors. Its shape evokes a cocoon, and has an undeniably dramatic presence. In 2015 a limited-edition version of this high-backed revolving design was created to mark Channels' twentieth anniversary, upholstered in two complementary fabrics from Osborne & Little's Amisi collection, designed by Nina Campbell.

110

ABC screen

Design Year: 2010
Material: American white oak
Measurements: 185 x 220 x 4 cm
Manufacturer: Channels, London

Every year since 2010, the global design magazine *Wallpaper** has paired a number of designers or artists with manufacturers in order to create special one-off pieces for it to show in Milan during the week of the famous Salone del Mobile. The resulting annual exhibition, 'Handmade', is, according to the magazine, a 'freshly minted celebration of craft, creativity and collaboration'. For the inaugural 'Handmade' in 2010, *Wallpaper** commissioned Channels to work with the graphic artist and printmaker Anthony Burrill, who is known for his bold slogan prints and geometric pattern-making. It was an inspired pairing that resulted in the ABC screen, named for Anthony Burrill and Channels. Samuel was responsible for the overall execution of the screen and the design of its frame, which includes wooden dowel hinges, and Burrill devised the cut-out landscape-inspired motifs that adorn the four panels. This collaborative design is testament to the remarkable carpentry skills of the craftsmen in Channels' workshop, for each of these complicated motifs has been precisely cut by hand.

'Contrary to appearances, the motifs on the screen are cut entirely by hand.'

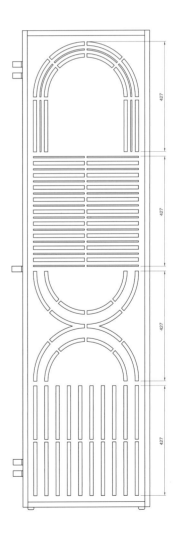

Three Wise Men bottle collection

Design Year: 2010
Materials: American white oak and American black walnut, white matte lacquer
Measurements: Various dimensions, 22–42 cm high
Manufacturer: Channels, London

'Sam loves wood-turning and wanted to make a few pure wood forms as accessories.'

Since childhood, Samuel has loved experimenting with woodworking tools to create shapes that express the intrinsic properties of the different types of timber he uses. In 2010 he created two collections of wooden bottles that did specifically that and were essentially highly refined formal explorations. These non-functional wooden pieces were intended first and foremost to be used as decorative accoutrements to his furniture designs, and certainly they look wonderful when grouped on one of his sideboards. Inspired by the gifts of the Magi to the newly born Jesus, this eye-catching trio of solid wood forms is named after the Three Wise Men – Melchior, Casper and Balthasar. Beautifully handcrafted in oak and walnut, they have cap-like stoppers with an off-white matte lacquer finish, helping to elongate the shapes of the bottles. The subtle contours of these bottles inspired the design of Samuel's later Three Wise Men pendant lights, which are made using a similar wood-turning technique.

Apothecary bottle collection

Design Year: 2010
Materials: American white oak and American black walnut, white matte lacquer
Measurements: Various, 24.5–38.5 cm high
Manufacturer: Channels, London

Samuel's second bottle collection, Apothecary, was also designed in 2010 and comprises five solid-wood forms crafted in oak and walnut, with oversized ball-like stoppers. With their bulbous abstracted forms, which obliquely recall the old-fashioned medicine bottles found in the pharmacies of yesteryear, the pieces were aptly named after five famous apothecaries and herbalists: Arnold, Bevan, Culpeper, Davy and Pemberton. Incredibly tactile and with a reassuring heft, these small sculptural forms invite the viewer to hold them and admire the subtle grain of their swelling surfaces.

Gillespie collection

Design Year: 2011
Materials
Tall glass cabinet: American white oak, glass
Side tables: American white oak or walnut, glass
Dressing table: American white oak with matte white lacquer on oak
Side chair: American white oak, wood-veneered plywood, wool felt
Measurements
Tall glass cabinet: 180 x 75 x 40 cm
Side table (small): 45 cm x 35 cm (dia.)
Side table (medium): 55 cm x 45 cm (dia.)
Side table (large): 65 cm x 55 cm (dia.)
Dressing table: 76 x 110 x 60 cm
Side chair: 79 x 45 x 45 cm
Manufacturer: Channels, London

According to Marylois, the Gillespie collection of cabinets, tables and seating 'reflects Samuel's perennial concern with achieving beauty, balance and discipline'. This collection, with its solid wood trumpet-shaped legs, was named as a tribute to the legendary American jazz musician Dizzy Gillespie, whom many consider to be one of the greatest masters of this versatile instrument. The flaring elements help to unify the collection stylistically across its different pieces – from its round pedestal side tables, with their glass 'doughnuts', to its elegant writing desk, and from its tall glass cabinet to its splay-legged chair – and give the range a very distinctive character and identifiable silhouette. This beautifully executed range is quite simply a tour de force of modern woodcraft.

'A contemporary exercise in precision woodworking.'

Gillespie rocking chairs + cobs

Design Year: 2010
Materials
Rocking chairs: American white oak and wool felt
Cobs: injection-moulded foam and wool felt
Measurements
Cob (small): 30 cm x 70 cm (dia.)
Cob (medium): 30 cm x 90 cm (dia.)
Cob (large): 35 cm x 110 cm (dia.)
Double rocking chair: 90 x 110 x 86 cm
Rocking chair: 90 x 50 x 86 cm
Manufacturer: Channels, London

When he was 15 years old, Samuel created his first 'design and make' furniture piece: a rocking chair for his mother. Many years later he created another simple rocking chair, the Gillespie, which is, by all accounts, a far more accomplished design. Available in two sizes – single and double – it has a solid oak frame with angled legs, and is upholstered in wool felt, as is so much of Channels' seating. An exercise in restraint and simplicity, this rocker – in spirit, at least – intentionally harks back to the historic rocking chairs made in Shaker communities across America in the late nineteenth and early twentieth centuries. Samuel's 'cobs', designed the same year, display a similar aesthetic purity. Described by Channels as 'informal, comfortable round forms', these sculptural, organic-form pieces can either be used as ottomans or brought into service as extra seats when needed.

Contour furniture range

Design Year: 2010
Material: American white oak
Measurements:
Console: 75 x 110 x 45 cm
Coffee table: 42 x 90 x 90 cm
Sideboard: 80 x 160 x 45 cm
Manufacturer: Channels for Heal's, London

Over the years, Samuel has designed several collections for Heal's, the famous British furniture and furnishings retailer that was founded in 1810 and has its flagship store on London's Tottenham Court Road. The firm has for decades been known for promoting stylish contemporary design, and in celebration of its two hundredth anniversary, in 2010, it launched a collection entitled Heal's ReDiscovers. As part of this initiative, not only were a number of 'classic' Heal's designs from the past reissued, but also several well-known British designers, including Samuel Chan, were invited to create new pieces that channelled the Heal's mid-century modern design spirit. Samuel's forward-looking yet craft-inspired Contour range for the collection contained four occasional pieces: an AV unit, a coffee table, a console table and a sideboard. Such pieces are usually typified by a certain angularity, but here Samuel explored more curvaceous forms made from thin looping bands of oak-veneered plywood that were painstakingly edged by hand with solid oak cross-band lipping and set on trumpet-shaped wood-turned legs of solid oak, a detail Samuel had introduced in Channels' own Gillespie collection the same year.

Monty collection

Design Year: 2011
Materials
Chairs: natural or stained American white oak,
plywood, wool felt
Multi-top tables: stainless-steel frame with leather top
or solid oak frame with oak top
Low tables: American white oak with matte colour top
Side tables: natural or stained American white oak
Measurements
Desk chair: 78 x 58 x 55 cm
Tall light: 185 x 45 x 45 cm
Multi-top table (two-top): 50 x 68 x 35 cm
Multi-top table (four-top): 50 x 81 x 76 cm
Manufacturer: Channels, London

The Monty collection began with a desk chair. Samuel had always wanted to design a swivelling chair with a pedestal base, but one that would not look too office-like and that would, therefore, be more suited for use in a domestic setting. Realizing that most desk chairs on the market had a rather mechanical, industrial aesthetic, Samuel decided to create something with a much softer, more crafted feel. With this aim, instead of using metal for the rotating pedestal base, as is traditional, he opted for wood – always his preferred material. Using natural oak, he created a rounded stem from which splayed four tapering feet, and to this pedestal he connected a felt-upholstered seat, shell moulded from oak-veneered plywood. The overall effect was perfectly pitched for his home-office brief. After designing the Monty desk chair, Samuel added a low, wider lounge-chair variant to the series. He then created two matching side tables with the same stem-like pedestal feature and tray-like tops. These were followed by a table that employed, again, the same rounded stem feature with multiple plate-like elements. Unusually, Samuel also designed a metal version of this table, which revealed his ability to work adeptly with a material other than wood.

Jumeirah Himalayas Hotel

Design Year: 2011
Location: Pudong, Shanghai
Client: Jumeirah Hotel Group

The remarkable Zendai Himalayas building on the Pudong in Shanghai was designed by the internationally renowned Japanese architect Arata Isozaki and is already widely acknowledged as a modern Chinese architectural landmark. Samuel designed the furniture for the hotel in the building – the Jumeirah Himalayas – probably his most creatively important hotel commission to date. Working to a tight deadline and sensitive to his client's worldview and sensibilities, Samuel put together a broad range of furniture designs that were wholly contemporary and incorporated Oriental elements in a subtle yet confident way. Having gained the client's seal of approval, Samuel's original commission was for the suites; this quickly progressed to his being asked to design furniture for all the bedrooms and then, once he had finished that brief, the public areas as well. For these high-profile spaces, Samuel created a number of wonderfully evocative rooms that fused a 'memories of China' sensibility with a sense of international contemporary hotel chic. Importantly, what these rooms showed was how skilful Samuel is at creating a strong sense of place, which is sadly all too often lacking in modern hotel spaces.

Right: Bespoke chairs and tables, Shang-High Restaurant

Far Right: Motley lamps, baton chairs and stools, and bespoke tables, lobby

Bespoke cabinet and chairs,
private dining room,
Shang-High Restaurant

Bespoke dining furniture,
Shang-High Restaurant

Clockwise from top left:
Bespoke chaises longues, Atrium
Motley baton drums and bespoke
furniture, Suite
Bespoke furniture scheme, Suite
Bespoke benches, Lobby

Finnieston collection

Design Year: 2012
Material: American white oak or American black walnut
(tabletops with matte lacquer in various colours)
Measurements
Bookcase: 182 x 80 x 35 cm
Console table: 80 x 180 x 45 cm
Tripod table: 60 cm x 45 cm (dia.)
Tallboy: 150 x 45 x 45 cm
Manufacturer: Channels, London

Launched at 'designjunction' during the London Design Festival in 2012, the Finnieston collection was designed to demonstrate how high-level contemporary woodcraft could be used to create furniture with 'a fresh aesthetic and playful spirit'. Comprising just five pieces originally – a console table with open side rails and an open box frame, an open-ended bookcase with unusual laterally sliding shelves, an elegantly soaring tallboy with seven drawers, a handy tripod folding table with differently coloured tilt-tops, and a family of lamps with scissor arms and turned wood shades – the Finnieston collection received widespread critical acclaim when it first appeared, thanks to its functional inventiveness and visual dynamism. But the range was also notable for the strong silhouette of each design. Often the best indicator of a so-called iconic design is whether or not it has an easily identifiable profile, and certainly all five of the Finnieston designs have strong and memorable outlines that powerfully reveal Samuel's masterful understanding of the crucial interplay between form and function.

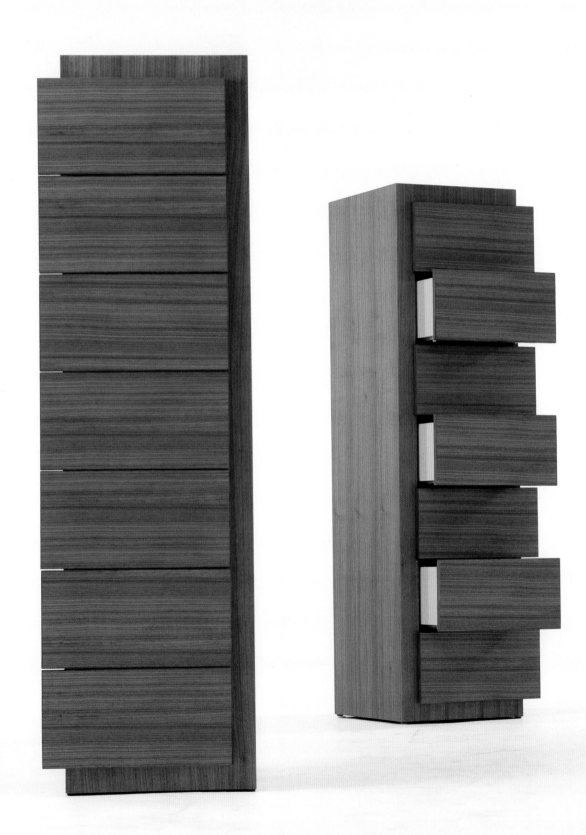

Finnieston lighting range

Design Year: 2012/2014/2015
Material: American white oak, American black walnut
Measurements
Floor light (standard): 152 cm x 35 cm (dia.)
Floor light (XL): 195 cm x 46 cm (dia.)
Desk light: 78 cm x 22 cm (dia.)
Chandelier (standard): 60 cm x 105.5 cm (dia.)
Chandelier (large): approx. 60 cm x 143 cm (dia.)
Manufacturer: Channels, London

The highlight of the Finnieston collection was without question Samuel's Finnieston lamp, which was launched in 2012. For, while referencing industrial task lights of the past with its adjustable scissor arm, it was very much a contemporary design that was feasible thanks only to advances in LED technology. As Samuel explained when the design was launched: 'This low-energy [LED] bulb – on the market just a few months – generates minimal heat, and means I could design an enclosed solid wood shade that wouldn't be damaged by the heat of traditional lamps. It's a detail I've always wanted to introduce – a solid wood, hand-turned shade and the warm light it gives.' Initially, the Finnieston was available as a floor light in two sizes and also as a desk lamp, but the design was so critically and commercially successful that Samuel revisited it in 2014, creating the extraordinary Finnieston chandelier and also a wall-mounted variant. In 2015 limited-edition versions of the Finnieston desk and floor lights were introduced to celebrate Channels' twentieth anniversary, featuring vibrant tangerine-coloured bases covered in high-quality leather sourced from the manufacturer Andrew Muirhead, and matching coloured cables.

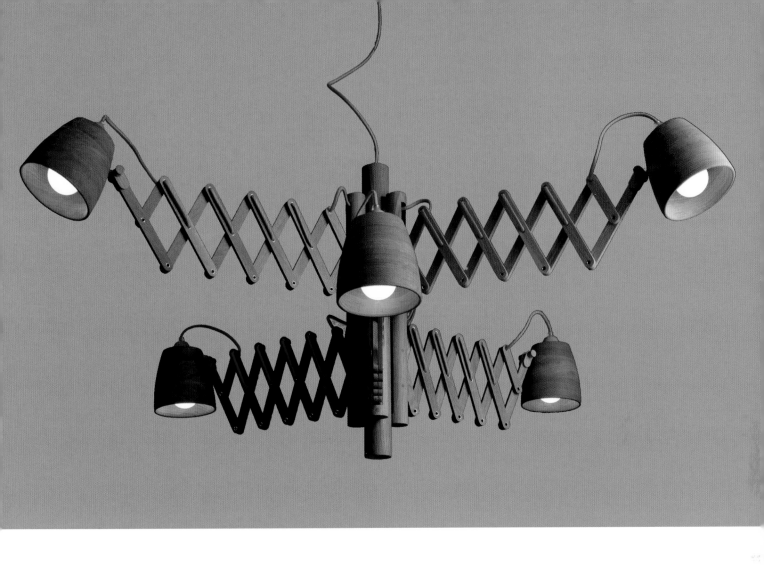

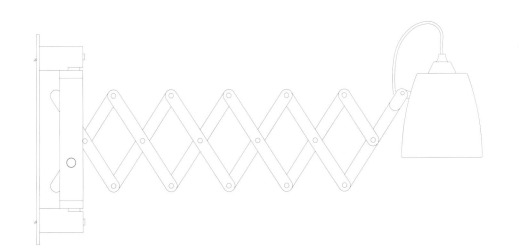

'The historic scissor-
mechanism lamp
made distinctive by
an extendable arm
carefully crafted
in wood.'

Three Wise Men pendant lights

Design Year: 2012
Material: American white oak or American black walnut
Measurements: Two sizes (standard/XL), various dimensions
Manufacturer: Channels, London

The first Three Wise Men design was for a trio of bottle-shaped wooden forms, created by Samuel in 2010. Two years later Samuel repurposed these enigmatic contoured forms for the design of three new pendant lights, which, like the earlier Finnieston lighting range, were made from hand-turned oak or walnut. Although they can be used singly, these three designs, which are individually named after the biblical Magi (Melchior, Casper and Balthasar) look their very best in clusters of three or more. In fact, in 2014 Samuel created a variant that grouped the three differently shaped designs within a balanced composition under a single ceiling rose, also made of wood. Each of the Three Wise Men pendant lights comes in two sizes, which can be mixed and matched.

Kerning collection

Design Year: 2014
Material: American white oak
Measurements
Sideboard (4 doors): 76 x 175 x 40 cm
Cabinet: 111 x 96 x 40 cm
Sideboard (2 doors): 66 x 86 x 40 cm
Tallboy: 146 x 46 x 40 cm
Bookcase: 200 x 100 x 32 cm
Manufacturer: Channels, London

After the establishment of Joined + Jointed in 2013, Samuel was deliberate in steering his own Channels studio to concentrate on what made it distinctive: designing one-off and low-volume production pieces made with high-value craft and featuring labour-intensive detailing. The Kerning collection is very challenging to make: for instance, from a distance the cabinet panels appear to be framed by a darker border, which is in fact a very precise gap of 15 mm, with the doors held in place by concealed round-dowel-peg pivoting hinges. The collection name is also a clue to understanding Samuel's approach: in typography, 'kerning' is the painstaking process of adjusting the spaces between characters. As well as playing with mathematical proportions, in the Kerning collection Samuel is also rethinking form and function: the Kerning bookcases, with their carefully spaced alternating shelves, have a distinctive visual rhythm and a light, floating aesthetic not traditionally associated with bookcase designs. They represent classic modern design with a twist. The American designer Charles Eames once famously said, 'The details are not the details. They make the design,' and this is especially true of Samuel's work. The Kerning cabinet series and bookcase series were given Design Guild Marks in 2015, and in the same year Samuel was named Furniture Designer of the Year at the *Homes & Gardens* Design Awards.

'Perfect proportions. Makes wood sing.' *Homes & Gardens* Design Award judging panel

20th Anniversary collection

Design Year: 2015
Material: various
Measurements: various
Manufacturer: Channels, London

In 2015, to celebrate Channels' 20th anniversary, Samuel chose three of his most distinctive designs and re-launched them as limited editions featuring new and exquisite finishes. The Hume book towers, first launched in oak in 2007, were now presented in walnut with contrasting interior panels of matte brass. The Motley tall baton chair of 2010 was upholstered in a luxurious combination of fabrics by Nina Campbell for Osborne & Little, and Samuel's iconic Finnieston lamps of 2013 were injected with colour with the addition of an orange cable and vibrant orange base made from Scottish leather supplied by Andrew Muirhead. Each limited edition design had a production run of 20.

Three Wise Men 2015 pendant lights

Design Year: 2015
Material: American white oak or American black walnut
Measurements: various dimensions
Manufacturer: Channels, London

There is an old saying that 'necessity is the mother of invention', and in many ways the 2015 edition of the Three Wise Men pendant lights was the result of a need to find a way of reducing the production costs of the original versions, the hand-turned shades of which made them relatively expensive to manufacture. Despite all his technical know-how, Samuel could not find a way to replicate the lights more cheaply. In the end he began to think about the design itself, and came up with an ingenious solution that would allow him to keep the profile shapes he loved, yet produce them at a more affordable cost. He essentially flattened the designs into silhouetted forms, which not only used significantly less wood, but also were far less labour-intensive to construct than their solid-wood hand-turned forerunners. Quite different in feel from the original Three Wise Men lights, which are still in production, this more edgy edition has a very distinctive graphic 'meta-design' quality.

Column bookcases

Design Year: 2015
Material: stained walnut
Measurements
Column I: 240 x 47.5 x 45 cm
Column II: 210 x 47.5 x 45 cm
Column III: 170 x 47.5 x 45 cm
Manufacturer: Channels, London

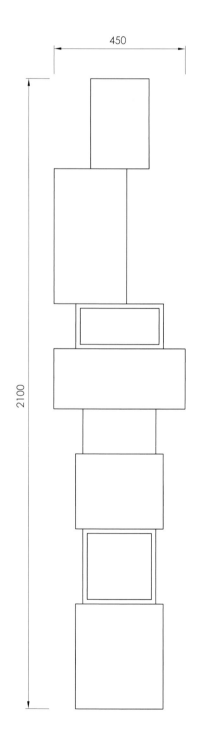

In 2015 – Channels' twentieth year – Samuel felt it was the perfect time to start exploring new sculptural possibilities that would push the creative boundaries of contemporary woodcraft. The three Column bookcases were one of the first results of this new direction, as a press release for their launch explained: 'Functionally, they work as 'storage pieces', but their value lies in their visual rhythm; whether individually or as a group, the rising blocks create a staccato effect that is also fluid and harmonious.' Statement 'design–art' pieces with a strong visual and physical presence, the Columns are strikingly accomplished in both overall concept and exacting execution. They testify to Samuel's mastery of furniture design and making over the last 20 years, for although they are very simply constructed – just a series of open-ended boxes stacked one on top of another – they possess a powerful sense of inevitability, which is always the mark of a good design. It is the type of design that makes one wonder why no one thought of it before.

'A series of three tall structures, resembling a stack of building blocks.'

Magnus chair

Design Year: 2015
Material: American black walnut
Measurements: 135 x 48 x 67 cm
Manufacturer: Channels, London

Samuel has always loved designing and constructing furniture that is challenging to make, and which tests his craftsmanship skills and those of his team. His high-backed Magnus chair, with its remarkable criss-crossing pattern of interconnecting solid wood pieces, is one such design, for each of its numerous joints is unique. And although the 'bird's nest' pattern might appear to be random, it was actually very carefully worked out by Samuel to produce the most harmonious composition he could find. Likewise, the proportional relationship between the soaring back section and the seat is mathematically precise in order to be as visually balanced as possible. This remarkable chair, the construction of which is a sort of taxing cabinetmaking puzzle, is unquestionably Samuel's most accomplished seating design to date, for it skilfully blends a very Eastern motif with Western craft traditions in order to create a powerful 'Chinese Modern' statement.

'With its tall back and sharp geometry, Magnus is a masterclass in precise, patient woodworking.'

480

1350

Twr y Felin Hotel

Design Year: 2015
Location: St David's, Pembrokeshire, Wales
Client: Retreats Group

The Retreats Group owns Roch Castle in Pembrokeshire, and has turned it into luxury holiday accommodation. Also in its Welsh portfolio are the luxury Penrhiw Hotel and the arty, chic Twr y Felin Hotel, both in St David's, close to the world-famous beaches of the Pembrokeshire coast. Samuel developed and made furniture for all three projects, most recently for Twr y Felin, which was sympathetically yet cleverly converted from an old windmill. It has recently been named as one of the top 25 hotels in Great Britain by *The Times*. Located opposite the Oriel y Parc national park visitor centre, it boasts 19 bedrooms and 2 suites, all of which are furnished with bespoke designs that exude a sense of understated yet thoroughly contemporary luxury. Retreats Group owner and chairman of Aedas, Keith Griffiths comments: 'With painstaking craftsmanship, design ingenuity and perfect detail from Samuel this furniture is the hallmark of his company and establishes the perfect retreat environment that we required.'

'Samuel Chan has imbued
Channels with his design
ingenuity, talent and demand
for perfection.' *Keith Griffiths,
Chairman, Aedas*

149

Tobias workbench

Design Year: 2016
Materials: American white oak
Measurements: 90 x 120 x 80 cm
Manufacturer: Channels, London

This exquisite workbench is named after Tobias Chan, Samuel and Shirley's younger son, and is intended primarily for men who enjoy making things at home as a hobby. It was Tobias's love of woodwork at school that prompted the initial design, which Samuel created as a surprise present for his twelfth birthday. It is still far too soon to say whether Tobias will follow in his father's furniture-designing and -making footsteps, but certainly there are not many schoolboys with such a beautiful workbench at which to hone their carpentry skills. When Samuel saw how well Mike France had translated his original working drawings into a perfectly crafted object, he thought other people might like to acquire their own luxury workbench, and so in 2016 he put the piece into production.

'Woodworking is an elemental thing. The challenge is to do something new with this ancient activity.'

Shoe Tree

Design Year: 2016
Material: walnut
Measurements: 230 x 44 x 44 cm
Manufacturer: Joined + Jointed, London

One of Samuel's latest creative collaborations was with the shoe designer Beatrix Ong, who, although British-born, spent her early childhood in Hong Kong. She returned to the UK, where she studied at Roedean School in Brighton before training as a designer at Central Saint Martins and London College of Communication. Like Samuel, Ong is famed for her 'classic with a twist' approach to designing shoes, so it is easy to see why *Wallpaper** magazine chose to pair the two, under the guise of Joined + Jointed, to collaborate on the design of a special one-off furniture piece to show at its annual 'Handmade' exhibition in Milan. It is also not surprising, given Ong's speciality, that the resulting design was for a shoe storage unit. Named Shoe Tree, this towering ladder-like structure with its 14 wooden shoeboxes is not only an eye-catching monument to the contemporary phenomenon of the designer shoe, but also provides efficient storage for a sizeable cache of footwear. This beautifully crafted design testifies to Samuel's ability to create functionally clever yet witty pieces that also have a powerful sculptural resonance.

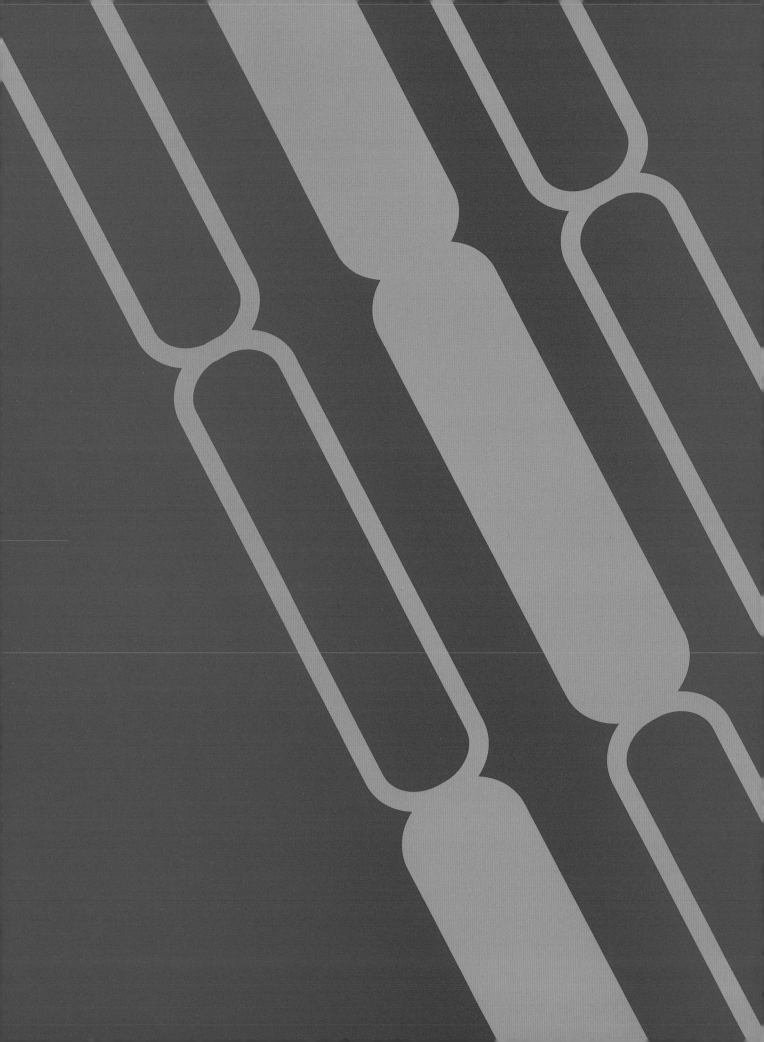

Joined+ Jointed

Creative
Collaborations

Founded in 2013 on the idea of 'creation through collaboration', Joined + Jointed is a relatively new furniture design–make–sell venture in which Samuel works in a more curatorial role. As well as being J+J's founding designer, Samuel also invites designers whose work he admires, and who come from a similar design–craft background, to contribute to the company's collections, which are made using artisanal production methods. Launched to bring well-designed and beautifully made, simple yet functional furniture pieces to online customers at an affordable price, Samuel's brainchild has already received an enormous amount of critical praise from the design press. Through the auspices of J+J, Samuel has managed to achieve something generations of designers before him have only dreamed of – to find a way of squaring high-quality design and manufacture with affordability. He has done this by adhering to his guiding ethos of twinning design purity with craft principles. By managing to attain that elusive trinity of good design, good manufacture and good price point, Samuel has in many ways achieved the central, yet unrealized, goal of the Arts and Crafts movement. The first contributors to this very different online furniture project include some of Britain's most established and prolific designers – Simon Pengelly, Alex Hellum, Rod and Alison Wales, and Marcus Beck and Simon Macro of Freshwest – as well as the American-born, Milan-trained designer Sean Yoo and the Danish designer Henrik Sørig. In 2015 the young but already accomplished designer Lucy Kurrein was added to the roster. All of them share Samuel's vision and are enthusiastic to have found a new channel for their work. Importantly, it is not just the design press that is impressed with J+J's furniture, but also its burgeoning customer base. For Samuel, as a designer-maker deeply committed to his craft, these are exciting times. He has finally managed to find a way of working at the highest level at both ends of the creative spectrum – the bespoke and the mass-market – without having to compromise his dedication to total design integrity.

Lazy chair by Freshwest, Homestation desk by Henrik Sørig, and Aponi bureau/dressing table by Lucy Kurrein – all for Joined+Jointed, 2013

Previous page: Trident armchair by Simon Pengelly, Trapeze by J+J Studio (Samuel Chan) and Incline side table by J+J Studio (Samuel Chan), all for Joined+Jointed, 2013 – shown with Finnieston floor light by Samuel Chan for Channels

Clockwise from left: Concave bookcase by Simon Pengelly, Wood III chair by Henrik Sørig, Jot desk by Alex Hellum, Span dining table by Wales & Wales – all for Joined + Jointed, 2013. All awarded Design Guild Marks

Pallet drawer system by
Samuel Chan and Willow
chairs by Sean Yoo, both for
Joined+Jointed, 2013

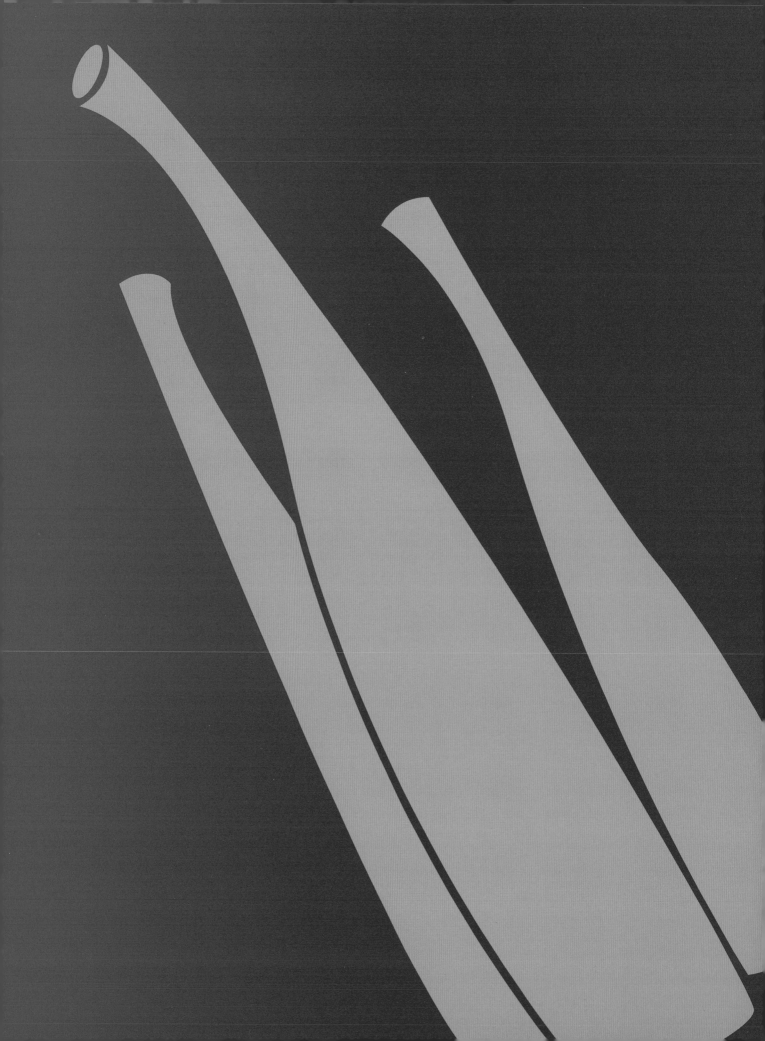

Additional
Designs
+Projects

Selected
Additional Designs

Alba sideboard 1
Design Year: 1988
Material: cherry
Measurements: 100 x 100 x 50 cm

Alba dining table
Design Year: 1995
Material: cherry
Measurements: 75 x 150 x 90 cm

Alba gentleman's wardrobe
Design Year: 1995
Material: cherry
Measurements: 220 x 96 x 66 cm

Wem bureau
Design Year: 1999
Material: walnut
Measurements: 164 x 100 x 50 cm

Wem side tables + cabinets
Design Year: 1999
Material: oak/walnut
Measurements: 60 x 45 x 45 cm

Wem side table with box
Design Year: 1999
Material: oak
Measurements: 90 x 60 x 40 cm

Memory cabinet I
Design Year: 1997
Material: oak/walnut
Measurements: 90 x 74 x 40 cm

Memory filing chest
Design Year: 1998
Material: oak/walnut
Measurements: 48 x 48 x 48 cm

Beka sideboard
Design Year: 1999
Material: cherry
Measurements: 80 x 150 x 40 cm

Wem X-frame side table
Design Year: 2000
Material: cherry
Measurements: 50 x 48 x 48 /
59 x 90 x 45 cm

Wem writing desk
Design Year: 2000
Material: cherry
Measurements: 77 x 100 x 55 cm

Zac diversion station
Design Year: 2000
Material: English sycamore
Measurements: 137 x 221 x 55 cm

Selected
Additional Designs

Zac side cabinet
Design Year: 2000
Material: English sycamore
Measurements: 40 x 60 x 40 cm

Juxa bar
Design Year: 2001
Material: oak
Measurements: 90 x 120 x 47 cm

Juxa high-backed chair
Design Year: 2001
Material: oak
Measurements: 100 x 52 x 52 cm

Paper bin
Design Year: 2003
Material: oak
Measurements: 35 x 28 x 28 cm

Boxes
Design Year: 2003
Material: oak/walnut
Measurements: various

Candlestick + vase
Design Year: 2003
Material: oak/walnut
Measurements: 20 x 6 x 6 cm

Juxa hat stand
Design Year: 2001
Material: oak
Measurements: 159 x 45 x 45 cm

Flyt dressing table
Design Year: 2002
Material: walnut
Measurements: 76 x 150 x 70 cm

Tot modular units
Design Year: 2003
Material: oak/walnut
Measurements: 80 x 80 x 40 cm

Wood forms
Design Year: 2003
Material: oak/walnut
Measurements: various

Motley I chest-of-three-drawers
Design Year: 2007
Material: oak
Measurements: 60 x 100 x 55 cm

Motley I chair
Design Year: 2007
Material: stained oak/leather
Measurements: 80 x 57 x 60 cm

Selected
Additional Designs

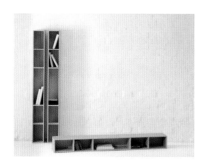

Motley I slim bookcase
Design Year: 2007
Material: oak
Measurements: 150 x 16 x 19 cm

Motley II sofa
Design Year: 2008
Material: oak
Measurements: 70 x 110 x 65 cm

Motley II armchair
Design Year: 2008
Material: oak
Measurements: 70 x 70 x 65 cm

Gillespie desk
Design Year: 2010
Material: oak
Measurements: 76 x 110 x 60 cm

Gillespie dressing table
Design Year: 2010
Material: oak
Measurements: 76 x 110 x 60 cm

Gillespie glass cabinets
Design Year: 2010
Material: oak
Measurements: 180 x 75 x 40 /
120 x 100 x 40 cm

Motley III oval dining table
Design Year: 2009
Material: oak
Measurements: 73 x 220 x 120 cm

Motley III side tables
Design Year: 2009
Material: oak/stained oak
Measurements: 45 cm x 35 cm
(dia.) / 55 cm x 45 cm (dia.) /
65 cm x 55 cm (dia.)

Motley III pendant light
Design Year: 2009
Material: oak/stained oak
Measurements: 50 x 50 / 60 x 60 /
80 x 80 cm

Gillespie side tables
Design Year: 2010
Material: oak/walnut
Measurements: 45 cm x 35 cm
(dia.) / 55 cm x 45 cm (dia.) /
65 cm x 55 cm (dia.)

Gillespie lamp table
Design Year: 2010
Material: oak/stained oak
Measurements: 135 cm x 45 cm
(dia.) / 165 cm x 55 cm (dia.)

Monty lounge chair
Design Year: 2011
Material: oak
Measurements: 64 x 58 x 62 cm

Selected
Additional Projects

Emmott Residence, 1997

MacLellan Residence, 2000

Mansfield Residence, 2000

The Langham, 2009

Grosvenor House Apartments,
2011

Penrhiw Priory, 2012

Hurrell Residence, 2001

Ettedgui Residence, 2003

Malmaison Belfast, 2003

Conrad London St James, 2012

Roch Castle, 2013

Ockenden Manor, 2014

Footnotes

Please note: All quotes attributed to Samuel Chan, Shirley Wong, Marylois Chan and Mike France come from a series of interviews conducted by Charlotte Fiell between December 2015 and January 2016.

Footnote 1: Joanna Watt, 'The State of Play', *Telegraph Magazine*, 11 April 1998.

Footnote 2: In 1945, Japanese rule ended and Hong Kong's sovereignty was returned to the British, which precipitated a mass-migration of refugees fleeing from the Communists on mainland China, so much so that Hong Kong's population rose from 750,000 inhabitants in 1945 to 2,200,000 in 1950.

Footnote 3: Rennie's Mill, also known as Tiu Keng Leng, was in the Sai Kung district of Hong Kong. In 1996, the Hong Kong government evicted the Nationalist-sympathizing 'squatter' residents of Rennie's Mill and their homes were cleared in order to make room for the building of a new town. It is widely believed, however, that this action was undertaken to appease the People's Republic of China who took control of Hong Kong the following year.

Footnote 4: The Free China Relief Association, a politically orientated charitable body run by the Kuomintang ostensibly took over the welfare of the Rennie's Mill district when the Hong Kong government suspended food rationing in 1953.

Footnote 5: Qingdao was originally a German concession established in 1898 after the Chinese were coerced by Germany into leasing 553 square kilometres of land for a period of 99 years. The Germans, however, remained in control of the territory for just 15 years, being defeated by Japanese forces in 1914. Nevertheless, it was the first European concession on mainland China, and, during their tenure, the German occupiers established a number of Christian churches there.

Footnote 6: St James' Primary School in Wan Chai, Hong Kong.

Footnote 7: In 2004, the Chinese Church in London relocated to Brook Green in Hammersmith.

Footnote 8: It is interesting to note that the pared-down aesthetics of Japanese Zen can actually be traced back to Chinese Taoist philosophy via Japanese Zen Buddhism.

Footnote 9: The beech found in the Buckinghamshire woods was traditionally used to make the well-known spoke-backed Windsor chair and other vernacular models. High Wycombe was also home to a number of well-known furniture manufacturers, including Hille and Ercol.

Footnote 10: Albert Isherwood & Company was first incorporated in 1909 and was subsequently dissolved in 2001. It was a big operation having its own joinery department, sawmill, drying kiln and timber-sales division. It was also the main supplier of butchers' blocks in Britain.

Footnote 11: The son of a joiner, Mike France had joined Albert Isherwood & Company directly after leaving school, at the age of 16, in order to learn 'the trade' (joinery). As Samuel notes, 'He has an ability to read the grain of a piece of wood, like nobody else I've ever seen.'

Footnote 12: It was not until his father died in 2010 that Samuel came to realize just quite what a huge undertaking it had been for his father to oversee the production in China. His father had left diaries detailing day-to-day operations during its first three years.

Footnote 13: This was later borne out, when in the middle of night Mei Tak was woken up by an extremely sudden and violent downpour heralding the start of monsoon season. He immediately jumped out of bed and rushed to the workshop fearing that it would be underwater, but much to his surprise 14 of 'his boys' had already got there and had moved all the furniture up on to the workbenches out of harm's way. He later phoned Samuel to recount this incident and said, 'It really shows they care, they must remain with us for as long as they want to be with us.'

Footnote 14: The Chinese-born evangelist pastor Stephen Wang founded the interdenominational Chinese Overseas Christian Mission in London in 1950. Its goal is to bring the Christian gospel to Chinese people living in Europe as well as to local Europeans through its multi-facet ministries.

Index

Main entries are indicated in **bold**
Images in *italic* on page image caption appears
  (or image appears, if no caption)
Designs are by Samuel Chan unless otherwise stated

Credits + Acknowledgements

We would like to offer heartfelt thanks to **Samuel Chan** for undertaking this project with us, and for sharing his fascinating design philosophy and personal story. Huge thanks must also go to Samuel's wife, **Shirley Wong**, and sister, **Marylois Chan**, for their invaluable additional insights into his work and their assistance with imagery and fact checking. We would also like to thank **Melissa Danny** at **Laurence King Publishing** for her good-natured editorial management of the project, **Sam Morley** for his beautiful graphic design work and patient inputting of last-minute changes, and **Kim Wakefield**, also at Laurence King, for her meticulous colour correction of the images.

Picture Credits

All imagery taken by Philip Vile, courtesy of Channels Design, except for the following:

p8 courtesy of Adrian Green
pp15, 62-63 Shirley Wong, courtesy of Channels Design
p29 portrait of Samuel Chan by Amy Boyd, courtesy of Channels Design
pp36, 38, 40, 44, 45, 47 Abdul Momin, courtesy of Channels Design
pp54-55 courtesy of The Trafalgar hotel, London, UK
pp68-69 courtesy of AvroKO, New York, USA
pp70-71 photos of Kong Fok Church, Hong Kong, courtesy of Channels Design
pp74-75 photos of The Tea Gallery, New York, USA, courtesy of Channels Design
p99 courtesy of Linteloo, Zeist, The Netherlands
p110 graphics courtesy of Anthony Burrill
pp118-119 courtesy of Heal's, London, UK
pp148-149 courtesy of Retreats Group, St David's, UK
p157 courtesy of Jonathan Gooch, styled by Kate-Louise Thomas
p170 photo of Grosvenor House Apartments, courtesy of Jumeirah International
p170 photo of Penrhiw Priory, courtesy of Retreats Group, St David's, UK
p171 photo of Conrad London St James, courtesy of Conrad Hotels
p171 photo of Roch Castle, courtesy of Retreats Group, St David's, UK
p171 photo of Ockenden Manor, courtesy of Historic Sussex Hotels, UK

Cover: Magnus chair (2015)
Page 1: Magnus chairs and Column bookcases (both 2015)
Both images photographed by Philip Vile, courtesy of Channels Design